THE HEART OF LOVE

Brian Pickett

The Heart of Love

Prayers of German Women Mystics

 St Paul Publications

ACKNOWLEDGEMENT: All the translations in this anthology are the author's own except those on pages 31 and 75, which have been slightly adapted from Carol North Valhope's translations published in *The Spear of Gold*, ed H.A. Reinhold, Burns & Oates, London 1947.

St Paul Publications
Middlegreen, Slough SL3 6BT, United Kingdom

Copyright © St Paul Publications UK 1991
Printed by The Guernsey Press Co. Ltd, Guernsey, C.I.
ISBN 085439 366 8

St Paul Publications is an activity of the priests and brothers of the Society of St Paul who proclaim the Gospel through the media of social communication

To my mother and father

Contents

Introduction

With all our heart

'That was a beautiful prayer', a voice called to me as I finished praying with one of my congregation. I crossed the hospital ward to meet a Jewess recovering from an operation, and, struggling to think of some appropriate response, I suggested we unite in saying the Hebrew *Shema*:

'Hear, O Israel: the Lord our God, the Lord is One.
And you shall love the Lord your God
with all your heart, and with all your soul,
and with all your might.'

(Deut 6:4-5; cf Mk 12:29-30)

It says it all. The oneness of God which we need to know and seek to show is found in the love of the heart. It is in the heart that we must stand before heaven and meet with God. Heart speaks to heart.

The heart here is not a souvenir shop of all our past sentimentality nor a barometer of our moods and emotions. It is the focus and centre of our whole life: our understanding and perception, our will and energy, our whole personality. The heart is where the Kingdom

1

comes, where God's will is done and heaven is found on earth, because the heart is where we offer our whole selves to God.

The Church needs the prayer of the heart more than ever. The sterility of traditions that have not grown and the barrenness that comes from liturgies which are modern, correct and comprehensible, yet devoid of any attractive beauty or numinous mystery, have driven many Christians to try to find the religion of the heart in a charismatic experience, often like the seed that grew too quickly without any depth of soil (Mk 4:5). Others have left formal religion to seek some meaning in poetry, art or music: we may feel they lack any firm commitment or direction in life, but their loss is also the Church's loss. We miss them as much as we miss those who find emotional fundamentalism represses their true doubts and feelings and leaves them disillusioned with easy answers to questions never faced.

In this anthology, women of God from mediaeval Germany offer us the prayer of the heart, committed emotionally and mentally to love of God with warmth and joy, celebrating that love with prodigal, and some-times erotic, poetry and song, yet finding love's mystery of joy and pain signed and sealed in the wounded Heart of the Crucified Christ. And always, the power of their emotion is earthed in the daily discipline of prayer and Sacrament and the faith in the undivided Trinity.

They set before us a feast of love, not just in the imagery of the heavenly Bridegroom and the earthly Bride, which we expect of mystics, but in a feminine insight into the nature of God. God's heart of love in their prayers does not master a subject world but moves redemptively from within it through creation, incarnation, and the new creation of Christ's cross and resurrection, drawing our hearts to become one with the heart of God.

Women's contribution to mediaeval spirituality has

2

until recently been overshadowed by the great male preachers like Bernard, Eckhart, Tauler and Francis. This reflects the lamentable neglect of provision for women of the period in religious life. It took the great reforming Cluniac tradition over a hundred and fifty years to found a convent for women, not least because they feared contact with women would contaminate their spiritual life and endanger any revival! Even the enlightened St Norbert of Xanten (1080-1134) who founded parallel houses for brothers and sisters from the start at Prémontré (1121) and later at Magdeburg, had his work destroyed by anti-feminist successors who scandalously abandoned the women's houses without any means of support. Yet, there is a treasury of women's spirituality waiting to be discovered. Much, including some of the material in this book, has not been translated into English before.

These prayers are the work of nine women. From the tenth century comes the first German woman writer known to us by name – Hroswith of Gandersheim, a nun with a remarkable gift for poetry and drama. Twelfth-century Rhineland boasts two Benedictine nuns – Hildegard of Bingen and Elisabeth of Schönau. Both received extraordinary visions from God, often in the liturgy, and made their prophetic voices heard against the corruption in the Church and its leaders. From the eastern part of Saxony, three nuns represent the 'crown of German cloisters' at Helfta near Eisleben, which Gertrude of Hackeborn (d. 1291) nurtured for forty years as abbess – Mechtild of Hackeborn was the choir mistress or 'nightingale' of the convent, Gertrude the Great, its greatest spiritual director, and Mechthild of Magdeburg, a visionary who took refuge at Helfta after suffering for her criticisms of the powerful. She brought with her the influence of the Beguines, to whom she had belonged. This was a community of lay women, originating in Liège, dedicated to meditation of Christ's passion, the eucharist and works of charity.

Another movement, from the fourteenth century, whose view of the equality of sexes helped women in their search for union with God through prayer, self-denial and the work of the Spirit, was the 'Friends of God', particularly active in Bavaria and Swabia and represented here by Margaret Ebner and Elisabeth Staeglin. Finally, from eastern Prussia (now Poland), we include Dorothea of Montau's eucharistic devotion, devotion wrung from the trials of a difficult marriage. More detailed biographies appear at the end of the introduction.

Some people feel that the prayers of great spiritual leaders are useless to ordinary Christians. Their train of thought is far too high-flown for us and does not touch our reality. The prayers of these women are certainly not untouched by the pain of sin or despair, loneliness or persecution. But the point is that prayer (like liturgy) is not just about expressing what we feel at any given time. If it is really prayer of the heart before the heart of God, then the Spirit is praying within us God's prayer, forming and moulding us in the image of God in Christ. The 'Our Father' is the classic prayer to help us pray, not our prayer but Christ's. Thus, the prayer of women who were so at one with Christ can help form Christ within us by the power of the Spirit who prays with us.

In our personal prayer, they may be our guide in times of despair and depression, encouraging us to find God's love (36, 45, 49, 51-3, 78, 83, 92-4). They knew what it was like to be powerless and vulnerable. They knew the hurt of betrayal and unkindness from those they trusted, even from the Church. They felt, as we do at times, that God is absent from our troubles (87, 92). They help us see our way through suffering and see causes for thankfulness and friends who love us, when our perspective is blinded by despair. There are prayers which will help us in preparing to make our Confession (91-2) and, in times of spiritual wilderness, when we feel in

Mechthild's words like 'an arid field where little good has grown' (92), the mystics turn our dry, wasting apathy into a positive thirst for the Fountain of life (58, 105, 108-110). In the coldness and numbness of our loveless hearts they make us pray for the warmth of God's love to burn up our dross and set us ablaze. They describe it as the warmth of a hearth that brings our frozen limbs back to life (*refocillare*) on a winter's day (51, 111). Gertrude's prayer on the Holy Spirit (68) and her exercises on 'Arousing the love of God' (105-7, 85-6, 88), are especially valuable in directing us away from the vortex of self-despair to a longing for God.

The eucharist, which fulfils all our longing, needs particular preparation in prayer, and the mystics' prayers encourage us to make the time and space to give all our attention to the heavenly Lover who comes to make us God's own in this wedding-feast. Together with the prayers to Our Lady and the Saints (51, 117-124), the eucharistic devotions (79-83, 105-114) offer us a preparation for Sundays and feast days, a preparation which requires planned time on our own – not a few minutes snatched in the rush before Mass!

Though this collection is not designed for children there are some prayers whose beauty and directness would be suitable for family prayer or school assembly (36-7, 50, 57-8, 70-2, 84-5, 91-2, 110).

For Church groups, the emphasis that the mystics place on healing will be helpful for prayer-cells who are committed to intercession for the sick (45, 49, 51-2, 65-9, 77, 95-8, 109). We shall discuss later the value of bringing our intercession to God with devotions to the Sacred Heart before the Blessed Sacrament. Apart from the beauty and stillness of the many prayers of adoration, there is a wealth of material for study-groups to meditate on: preparing for the Bridegroom in Advent (77-80, 92-3, 101, 120-2), empathising with the gospel stories in Hildegard's meditations (45-7, 49, 51-3), contemplating the Sacred Heart in Passiontide or at benediction (53-59), sharing Mechtild of Hackeborn's prayers on the 'joys of Christ in the resurrection' (60-1, 124), or praying for the work of the Spirit within us and the Church (65-72).

A special set of Gertrude's prayers focuses on our baptism and forms a good preparation for parents seeking baptism for their children. They take us through each symbol-signing (57), water (58), chrism (70), signing (59), light (59), Confirmation (71) and Communion (112-113). Their credal foundation and stress on ongoing discipleship make them ideal for use with the whole congregation or on retreats.

Religious communities will be able to use all this anthology to the full, but the prayers written for the Daily Office – Mechthild's prayers on the passion (54-6) and Gertrude's meditations on arousing the love of God (105-7, 85-6, 88), may be helpful resources on special occasions. Gertrude also wrote several renowned spiritual exercises for recollection on the anniversary of one's religious profession, some of which are reproduced here (32-3, 70-2, 77-80, 82-3) for their single-minded dedication of the whole heart to the Love of our heart.

One with our lover

From the most primitive rituals of sacred marriage onwards, our relationship with God has been expressed as a union comparable with that of lovers. In the Hebrew and Christian traditions this spirituality has developed beyond magical rites to preserve the earth's fertility to a committed covenant of love.

There can be no love without desire. We must want God, long for God with our whole heart. We must want our divine Lover to notice us and be drawn to stay with us and want us, just as we feel drawn by the attraction of God's grace. Such a reciprocal relationship needs cherishing and nurturing: above all it needs our time and attentiveness. It must also be redeemed from a mere desire for our wants to be satisfied – which is not a desire for the other person at all – and seek only to please God and find our fulfilment in loving God. Much of our prayer is far removed from this. In fact, it is really lust: we want God for the goods on offer – health, prosperity, comfort, assurance and power – but we do not really want God to be our lover for love's sake, only for what can be given to us.

Yet God desires us as we are, sinners *and* children of the divine image. God sees us in love, the love through which we were created, and desires us for love alone. God takes the initiative in showing us the love which is at the heart of our relationship. This is the foundation of all our evangelism. It is quite useless to ask repentance of people unless they first know of God's love. Only the knowledge of being loved can make us see the hurt we have caused God. Love is not the reward of repentance, still less of being 'good': it is a precondition of being able to repent at all.

Even then our relationship with God cannot be a purely personal indulgence but needs to be lived and shared in obedience to God's larger purpose for all the Church, where our union with God is fully consummated. Taking God's love without a commitment to Christ's body is like a love affair without a marriage.

The women mystics teach us that prayer is love. Their prayer encompasses a whole tradition of becoming one with God in love, wedded to God for eternity. By looking at that tradition here, we can understand that the mystics are not an eccentric oddity but carry within them the very heart of the faith.

In Hebrew Scripture, God's people are the beloved (Deut 33:12; Jer 11:15; Ps 60:5, 108:6, 127:2), betrothed in love (Hos 2:19-20; Ezek 16:8). The prophets describe the Lord as a deserted spouse who searches for the people

7

to be a bride again (Hos 2:16; Jer 31:32). The exiled Israel, like a wife forsaken, is assured that the Lord will bring her back, for her husband is also her Maker (Is 54:5): she shall be clothed with a bridal dress and the land itself will be wedded to God (Is 61:10-62:5). Another tradition celebrates the love of a royal bride and her king, anointed by God (Ps 45). This royal language of love is drawn upon in the Song of Songs to grace the romance of ordinary lovers, though its attribution to Solomon has gained a rich liturgical use for this imagery, as the Jewish custom of greeting the Sabbath as a bride illustrates.

The ambiguity of interpretation in the Song of Songs between the cultic and the personal has been a deep source of inspiration for Christian mystics who have seen the bride and bridegroom (like the eucharist) both corporately as a symbol of Christ and the people of God and individually as the relationship between God and the soul. Christ's own claim to be the bridegroom in whose presence the disciples find joy (Mk 2:19-20; Jn 3:29), and the parables of the kingdom consummated in the Messianic wedding feast (Mt 22:1-14, 25:1-13; cf Apoc 19:7,9) may have led the apostles to describe the Church as the bride (Eph 5:32; Apoc 21:2,9).

It is in the liturgy that we find the union of this love most fully expressed. Although the Song of Songs is lavishly applied to the Virgin Mary, she exemplifies our relationship with God. Throughout Orthodox prayer, the Lord is celebrated (as in Hildegard) as the lover of humanity (*philanthropos*). All the attentive expectancy of lovers is urged upon us in the Midnight Office and throughout Holy Week as the Church prays: 'Behold, the bridegroom comes!'. In Western liturgy many hymns focus on the Church as the Bride of Christ, notably the seventh century *Urbs beata Hierusalem* which sings of the bridal intercourse with the Lord (*Praeparata ut sponsata copuletur Domino*).

The fruitful union is liturgically consummated in the

mystery of Easter when the *Exsultet* proclaims the blessed night 'when heaven is wedded to earth' and the Paschal candle – the light of Christ – is plunged into the baptismal waters of the Church's womb. The same union is expressed individually in the Roman Pontifical's consecration of virgins: the nun is clothed, veiled and betrothed with a ring to words from the Song of Songs – 'Be betrothed, beloved, come, the winter has passed, the turtle dove sings, the vineyards burst into blossom... I betrothe you to Jesus Christ as a bride of God.'

The greatest writer of the mediaeval period to explore our personal communion with God was St Bernard of Clairvaux (1090-1153), who constantly urged his hearers to let themselves be 'affected' or moved by the Word of God in Christ, comparing this to the relationship of lovers. As Christ the spouse comes to visit the soul, the soul must lose all sense of present concerns and become inebriated with God's love until she begins to love God, for, 'if she loves God perfectly, then she is wed to God'.[1] For Bernard, love was not only charity or loyalty but charity seasoned with the very wisdom of God. Love as wisdom is also important to the women mystics, both as unfolding the power and purpose of God and helping the believer to grow. A contemporary of Bernard, Richard of St Victor (d. 1173), defined that growth in terms of a spiritual journey moving through four degrees of burning love – betrothal, marriage, the intercourse of prayer and the fruitfulness of spiritual creativity.

The renaissance of this spirituality in France coincided with the moral renewal of chivalry, and a flowering of the poetry of courtly love. The ideal of homage in love is perfectly illustrated in the Arthurian romance *Lancelot* (c. 1180) by Chrestien de Troyes, though some poets like Guiraut Riquier came to see the only proper subject of such verse as the Virgin Mary.

At Whitsuntide in 1184, German poetry took inspiration from a glittering ceremony at Mainz when the

9

emperor Barbarossa made his two eldest sons knights with all the pageantry and etiquette of chivalry. Courtly love (*Minne*) was no longer a French fashion but a German institution. Gone were the bawdy songs of wandering scholars like those in the Bavarian *Carmina Burana*. Now Minnesänger, like Walther von der Vogelweide (c. 1170-1228), developed an exuberant love poetry, full of wit but permeated with a spiritual quality beyond selfish desire. Where *triuwe* (loyalty) was the moral ideal in politics, *minne* became the ideal in personal morality.

St Francis made this genre his own in his courtship of Lady Poverty but the influences upon the mystics at Helfta came from contemporary German love poetry, inspired by the example of Flemish Beguine sisters like Hadewijs of Brabant (fl. c. 1221-1240), who contained all the passion of love for God within the courtly ideal of a knight's 'service' to the beloved.

This influence is reflected in the difference between Hildegard and Mechthild of Magdeburg. Hildegard's strongly sensual view of God's activity embraces all creation and her eroticism is focused on the incarnation, whether in the divine drink poured into Mary's womb (117) or the priest incarnating the Word made flesh on the altar (SACR 76). Her hymns on the saints (122-4) also delight in the warm intimacy of heaven. For her, the personal relationship is subsumed in the corporate and cosmic. Mechthild, however, enjoys the personal intimacy of divine courtship. Drawing on the dialogue of lovers in the Song of Songs, she fills her poems with the exchange of mutual compliments and extravagant praise. Image upon image of taste, scent and radiance (75-7) is depicted by God and the bride to mirror each other's qualities. Dancing, embracing and caressing (76, 78-9) are all natural expressions of the couple growing together. In seeking praise from God, Mechthild reveals her own insecurity, exacerbated by the persecution she suffered at Magdeburg, yet this faltering quest for love and security is all the more valuable to us in our own uncertainties.

A more confident approach to God appears in Gertrude, perhaps because her early entry into the convent shielded her from Mechthild's world. The homage of courtly love overflows into Gertrude's sense of wonder that God could have chosen her (77, 81, 83), but alongside the personal ecstasy she praises that same condescending love for all earth's children (33). Her lavishly erotic imagery is a remarkable witness to the depth of spirituality that Helfta nurtured. Surrounded by the warmth of her Love's embraces, she longs that her Love should have her and drench her with the Spirit's dew (82). When visited by the Lord at Christmas (at the Mass?), she feels the oil of God swelling and surging within her (83). All the language of love-making (*connubium, copulatio, consummatio*) is brought into play to express the oneness she experienced with God her Love.

Now these women were not repressed hysterics, separated from the company of men. Hildegard argued furiously with the monks of Disibodenberg for more space and independence but she valued her close relationship with Volmar, her secretary and confidant for thirty years. Mechthild of Magdeburg and Elisabeth Staeglin both sustained long and fruitful relationships with their spiritual directors. Nor were the convents as isolated as we imagine: Schönau was a double monastery where Elisabeth could lean out of the window and talk to the monks whom she knew by name. Helfta was protected by the relatives of Gertrude and Mechtild of Hackeborn and their intervention was often needed to ward off the greed of jealous barons. Moreover, the abbeys were besieged by visitors who came for counsel and liturgical nourishment. The balanced life of the mystics, whose convents protected them from the worst

11

of the Church's corrupt life and worship and also from its sexual stereotyping and suspicion, brings us a wealth of mature understanding of love. Thus, Mechthild comes to be thankful for the silences and absences which may just as eloquently speak of God's will (86-7). Her deprivation is a greater opportunity for grace, for, as she says, 'the deeper I fall, the sweeter you taste' (*VLG* IV.12).[2]

To our age where everything has its price, and relationships are often a matter of convenience and ambition (as indeed they were in their day) the love of these women for God must seem very strange. The lack of poetry and courtship in secular love is reflected in the dearth of beauty in our liturgy and the resistance to spending time courting God. Yet Gertrude's series of meditations on 'Arousing the love of God' have much to teach us about kindling that mutual desire without which love is a formality. Moreover, it is in that reflection on how God loves us that we discover our attractiveness and worth to God and ourselves. We learn, too, that love is a school, a growth which needs the time and space of courtship. Such a depth of knowing each other requires a readiness to be open and vulnerable to each other. Here the mystics also are not afraid to be frank and open in the offering of their whole heart to God, for they recognise that God is the only life we have (81). This contrast with our response to God hedged about with conditions and exemption clauses makes the prayer of the mystics even more vital in re-forming our spirituality.

For us, as for the mystics, the eucharist is the place where our eternal Lover comes into our hands in all the vulnerability of that gift, and we offer our vulnerability in our hands and heart open to the wounded heart of God. The drop of water poured into the chalice, which is our fragile human life, swells into the wine-red ocean of God's love. In this union, we become indistinguishable from God, one with all the love, the beauty and the glory of God in Christ. We are wedded to Christ at the altar in an eternal marriage. Christ's flesh is our flesh: our flesh is Christ's. The love of God is consummated in our body, for we are the Body of Christ, and yet our Communion is only the beginning of a new life.

We have seen how the mystics prepared themselves in prayer for this encounter. Our casual attitude to preparing for our Communion gives the world little clue as to whom we expect to meet, how great a guest, how generous a host, how devoted a lover. These prayers may help us give time and space to prepare for Christ, and to grow in our desire to be one in love with God.

Wounding and healing

The mystics found a special insight into their relationship with God in the 'wounding' of the beloved by the Divine Lover. Hebrew tradition understands the wound which God causes as a judgement, even though it brings eventual healing (Ps 51:8; Hos 6:1; Job 5:18; cf Heb 4:12), for God's judgement is motivated by love (Prov 3:12; cf Heb 12:6). Thus the pain of the beloved is the pain of God's love: the wound of the Daughter of Zion is the wounded heart of God (Jer 8:21); the wounds of the Suffering Servant are the Lord's will (Is 53:10); the sword that pierces the heart of God's Christ on the cross will pierce Mary's heart (Lk 2:34-35). For Paul also, to encounter Christ's sacrificial love is to have his own life crucified and subsumed within the life of Christ (Gal 2:20).

Many Christian writers have interpreted the wounding of the beloved both as a purging of sin and an identification with the pain of God's love. Origen writes of 'the saving wound' we receive when the splendour of Christ, our Spouse, overwhelms us with a burning fire. St John Cassian, whose writings greatly influenced Benedictine and Cistercian spirituality, urges us to seek the wound of contrition and, through self-renunciation, find union with Christ crucified. The seventh-century St Isaac of Syria encourages his hearers to desire the physical sign of repentance – 'the gift of tears'. This gift was especially revealed to another mystic, St Symeon the New Theologian, whose visions of the fire of God's love piercing his sin brought him continued weeping. This paradoxical sign of fire and water, reminiscent of baptism, not only purified but aroused a fresh thirst for God in him. In the West, St Bernard of Clairvaux was the greatest exponent of this mystery of joy and pain, describing how our Lover 'moves and warms and wounds the heart – hard and stony and sick though it be'.[3] While Mechthild of Magdeburg agonizes over the pain of our sin which causes God's pain (54-6), Gertrude (57) and Margaret Ebner (91) recognise the pain of Christ's wounds inscribed and imprinted on their heart. Hildegard describes it as the work of the Holy Spirit, purging us in the fire, wounding and breaking us in our sin (67).

Like Peter, we can only be healed by coming face to face with the one whom we have wounded. It is ironically the victim who has the sole power to heal us by the wounds we have caused. Thus Peter himself challenges the Jerusalem crowds at Pentecost to turn to 'this Jesus whom you crucified' (Acts 2:36) as their only hope of being healed. In any reconciliation we have to restore that part of the memory we would rather forget, and painfully return to our victims for forgiveness. Hence, amnesia is the first defence of the war-criminal. But Christ's work is about healing the memory and the relationship and is therefore inevitably a wounding experience. It is the painful drink that makes us healthy (109). Mechthild's prayers on the passion (54-6) make a particularly deep effect if, as we gaze with her at the crucifix, we picture on that face of Christ the victims we have hurt. We see Christ's image in them – and Chrisr's love for them and us. We also see ourselves, for we are made in that same image of God and by our sin we have hurt ourselves. Here pain is not resentfully hoarded to fester within us but freely carried and forgiven by the wounded Christ who makes us whole by accepting us and helping us accept ourselves.

This therapy is already understood in the unique suffering servanthood of Israel (Is 53) whose punishment makes us whole. The wound of love pierces and cleanses by the pain of self-giving love. For the mystics, penance could never be just a monetary restitution or an ascetic discipline but the penetration of love to save the heart from languishing in hurt or apathy. Anselm saw that the love that pierces the heart not only cleanses the past but moves the focus from self to Christ. The wound creates a new humanity that could never have been known without the brokenness that caused it. So, Mechthild speaks of being born from Christ's wounded side (34). With the living water from that wound comes the anointing of the Spirit which seals our forgiveness (70) and, in Hildegard's words, changes our wounds into precious jewels (67). From this experience the mystics developed a mature understanding of pain producing faith and even thankfulness (87, 96).

The penetrating wound was often seen as an expression of the incarnation, illustrated in the mediaeval legend of Christ the Unicorn lured to rest his horn on a virgin's lap. Gertrude indeed describes her Lord's visitation at Christmas in this erotic way, but the overwhelming influence of Beguine spirituality identified the penetrating wound with the crucified Christ. Mechthild prays to be made inseparably one with the wounded Christ, and physically sense the joy of that wounding (54-6), while Gertrude asks that her heart may be transfixed by Christ's pierced heart so that she may be possessed by God alone (57). As with other prayers that desire the beloved to be possessed, the image of bonding and belonging from love-making is transferred to the eucharist. Frequent

Communion was a hallmark of the Beguines' devotion to the passion.

Our approach to Communion may well have lost that sense of bonding and sharing in the life of God, and the prayers of the mystics, with their strong feeling of desire and commitment, help us in our preparation to make an offering of our whole selves when the priest bids us lift up our hearts.

As Christ was incarnate in the eucharist at the priest's hands, so some mystics, like Marie of Oignies (1176-1213) were led to receive the crucified Christ not only inwardly with the host, but outwardly with Christ's wounds imprinted on their own body. It was after receiving her Communion that Gertrude felt herself lying on the Lord's breast, 'as if about to be impressed with a seal'.[4] She seemed to be drawn into that treasury of love and receive an indelible mark of the Trinity. Like Paul, inwardly crucified to the world in baptism but outwardly bearing the marks of Jesus (Gal 6:17), Gertrude asks that the cross of baptism may be in her heart as on her forehead, and that Christ crucified may always be fixed there (58, 59).

For St Francis, the vision of 1224 when he received the stigmata was the climax of his desire to share the life of Christ. His solidarity with Christ's poverty and pain drew him to challenge the powerful and befriend the outcast. Receiving the wounds of Christ marked his own acceptance of that self-giving love for others. He reflects Paul's remarkable claim to 'complete in the flesh what is lacking in Christ's sufferings' (Col 1:24), continuing Christ's redemptive work through the Church.

The heart of Jesus to which we are wedded is the heart of God reconciling the world. The world's suffering is ours, because it is Christ's: that is the mystics' calling and ours. Thus, Isaac of Syria tells of 'the heart on fire for the whole of creation'.[5] Gertrude prays that Christ's wounds may arouse the pain of compassion in her and, as

Mechthild praises Christ's sacrifice as a fruitful pledge redeeming the world, she asks that her own daily life of self-denial may bring good to all. Of all the blessings flowing from the Sacred Heart, her dearest prayer is for the conversion of sinners (95, 114). In one vision she claims to have had her side pierced, and by this wound to have gained release for souls in purgatory.[6] It is surely no coincidence that this devotion to the Sacred Heart in Germany followed a renewed interest in the quest for the Holy Grail. Significantly, in Wolfram von Eschenbach's *Parzival* (c. 1210), the knight's great sin is to ignore the meaning of the bloody spear in the castle hall, and fail to enquire of Anfortas the meaning of his wounds.[7]

Love in the Christian life, however ecstatic, can never be separated from its fruitfulness in finding Christ in others. Though we may think her extreme, Mechthild of Magdeburg was quite unable, like Gertrude and others, to accept the concept of souls lost in hell, and she drove herself to pray constantly for friends and enemies alike. In the affluence of Western Christendom today, there is an absence of such urgency, and an unwillingness often to share the pain of the lost. But to turn our intercessions into just another parish notice-sheet, and leave it at that, is a poor response to the command to love our neighbour. We need to bring our intercession closer to the Sacred Heart as much for committing ourselves to be re-created in love for others as for those for whom we pray. A personal act might be to take someone needy in our heart to Church and offer them in prayer with ourselves at our Communion. On a corporate level, the Prussian churches at the time of Dorothea of Montau often left the Blessed Sacrament exposed in vigil for a day at a time. Let us pray in the sacramental presence of our Lord and learn how to love others and offer them in intercession, as we contemplate the tender heart of our great High Priest.

The femininity of God

The mystics' perspective on the world springs both from the suffering of Christ and from their common vision of the same heart of love at the source of creation. God is the life of every living thing forged with the divine spark of fire and sustained with eternal light. As their outspoken criticism of Church and society shows, they had no illusions about the destructiveness of sin, but they offer us a unitive view of humanity and the cosmos: God made the earth to be good, whole and holy, and God unconditionally enfolds all creation with love.

Their hymns and prayers celebrate this beauty with all the joy of the Hebrew prophets visualising the Messiah's world of peace and fruitfulness or the psalmist's orchestra of creation praising the Lord. Their prayer of created beauty has so much to offer modern church buildings which speak of convenience and function rather than the tracery of trees, and can enrich liturgies which have forgotten that every Christian festival grew from a Jewish harvest. Here is none of that fearful contempt for the world that we find in the contemporary Bernard of Cluny or the subsequent centuries of Calvinism.

Hroswith marvels at the distant constellations of the sky and the littleness of raindrops, all held in God's grasp. Hildegard sings of the Rhineland's craggy rocks and lush vineyards. Hers is a world of clear fountains, sun-baked fields and harvests, pastures wet with dew, and the earth dripping with moisture. She even treasured gold and precious stones, defending her nuns wearing them on feast days in praise of their Creator! Mechthild of Magdeburg finds joy in the nightingale's song and the flight of the dove, the lilies of the valley beside the river and the beauty of the rose. She makes her prayer in love and need in the fellowship of all God's creatures (50, 56), and with that community she joins her praise (95). For all the mystics, the universe is encircled by the dazzling and creative light of God. How much our narrowly thematic liturgy and even narrower selfish prayers need the cosmic breadth and belonging of their praises!

Neither did they shy away from the bodily sense of touch, celebrating, as we have seen, the relationship of the lover and the beloved with caressing, embracing and love-making. As the eucharist is the physical sign of this love, we naturally find taste to be a rich source of imagery. Gertrude, in particular, often makes the refreshment of eating and drinking express the pleasure of companionship with its richness (*pinguedo*) and sweetness (*suavitas*) of taste. Her desire is to kiss the honey-sweet lips of God and be incapably drunk under the influence!

If this unitive vision and sensuous enjoyment of creation are not distinctively feminine, the importance the mystics give to the nurturing of the Creator certainly is. Their prayer moves us away from a hierarchical view of a distant God to the God who touches and tends the earth, moving alongside us and within us. Hildegard sees the Holy Spirit's energy of love moving the flow of the clouds and the water in the brooks. God's nurture of creation is a metaphor for the growth of virgins in the warmth of the Sun, the evangelist planted by the heavenly gardener or the fruitful roots of the prophets. Gertrude also describes her spiritual growth as a fruit needing to be drenched by God's dew. For Mechthild of Magdeburg this growth stems from Christ's own passion which is the fruit of a fair flower.

In Mary nature and metaphor are one, as she fulfils the promise of fertility: she is the 'prime matter' (*materia* 117) who becomes the mother (*mater*), the virgin (*virgo*) soil from which the branch (*virga* 118) of faith flowers. Her womb brings forth the new creation, giving corn for the feast of the Messiah. Hildegard reflects this fertile growth by her distinctive use of the word *viriditas* – a green freshness (65, 117-8, 123) expressive of the holistic view of life echoed in her manuals on medicine and her use of herbs and Rhine water to heal the sick. Her approach finds an increasing resonance with our own ecological concerns.

Motherhood, the natural image of nurture, has a rich tradition in most ancient religions. In the Hebrew Scriptures, the Lord is like an eagle fluttering over her young, carrying them on her wings (Deut 32:11). God's love is compared to a nursing mother (Is 49:15), comforting Jerusalem that she in turn may satisfy the mourners from her consoling breasts (Is 66:10-13). Jesus' own longing was to gather the children of Israel together 'as a hen gathers her chicks under her wings' (Mt 23:37), inspiring Anselm to call Jesus 'our Mother'.[8] For the apostles the word of Christ is milk for the faithful to suck (1 Cor 3:1-2; 1 Pet 2:2). Hence, Aelred of Rievaulx bids us go to Jesus and draw 'the milk of consolation from the breast of the one who is mother to you'.[9]

The German mystics take the image of breast-feeding for God's nourishment of all creation, using the Latin *uberis* from the word for 'teat'. In the Pauline tradition of the cosmic Christ who gathers all things together (Col 1), it is the incarnate love of God who abounds in seeds that suckle life's fruits (33); it is Christ, the eucharistic bread of life, who suckles all earth's creatures (108, 114). Nurturing, of course, is a vital role of the Virgin Mary, and mediaeval iconography often depicts her as 'Maria lactans'. The mystics understood this image not only as one of tenderness but of strength: Mechthild of Magdeburg visualises Mary fortifying martyrs, penitents, oppressors and sinners alike with the milk of Christ's sacraments (119). But the mystics go further and depict God nurturing us, both in tenderness and power. Hildegard urges the faithful to suck justice and holiness from the breast of the Creator (39), while Gertrude seeks the intimacy of feeding from Christ, her love (86, 106). Her prayers could be illustrated from many mediaeval pictures of Christ offering the nourishment of the eucharist from the breast, including one in a manuscript of Hildegard. Hildegard, indeed, attributes the inspiration to write her 'Book of Divine Works' to the same Spirit which filled St John the evangelist when he sucked deep revelations from the breast of Jesus (cf Jn 13:23).

They did not rest, however, with these traditionally feminine insights into the creativity of God. Their rejection of a hierarchical god led them to prefer qualitative names for God such as Godhead (*Deitas/Gotheit*), Trinity (*Trinitas/Drivaltekeit*), Love (*Caritas/Minne*) and Tenderheartedness (*Misericordia/Barmherzekeit*). The feminine gender reflects a mystical reticence about defining God, but it also expresses the mystics' experience of the God who transcends traditional roles of gender. Thus, in Hildegard's hymn on the Trinity (32), she shows the omnipotent and initiating power of God as a feminine attribute by using the word *creatrix*. For Gertrude, the Trinity is also the source of feminine qualities such as wisdom, insight, love, sweetness and holiness (32). Power (*vis, virtus*), too, is understood as a feminine force, not manipulative or dominating, but creatively moving from within the world through the miracle of the incarnation (35, 44), holding us in the security of God's love. Hildegard identifies this 'life-giving life' with the energy of the Holy Spirit (66).

This exploration of the femininity of God has its roots in the Jewish Scriptures where Wisdom is portrayed as a feminine persona (Prov 8; Wis 7-9; Sir 24): she is the breath of God's power, encircling and counselling the world from eternity, the bride who shares the inmost thoughts of God, the fruitful tree whose produce nourishes the wise.

In Hildegard's visions the richness of God is revealed in an array of female forms. Wisdom (*sapientia*), dressed in the green of fruitfulness and the gold of obedience, plays and dances before God, embracing all creation in the harmony of heaven (35, 39-40). Love (*caritas*), the lady of the universe, rests in the centre of the wheel of eternity, revealing the life and beauty of God, for she embraces the king of all (31). The strength of care and compassion appears as Tenderheartedness (*misericordia*) dressed as a nun. She is the heart of Christ who meets the woman taken in adultery (53); she is the heart whom Gertrude asks to send the Holy Spirit of renewal (70). Two female figures appear in Hildegard's visions in holy orders. Knowledge (*scientia*) teaches sinners in the dazzling vesture of a bishop, while the Church (*ecclesia*) – who, like Wisdom, exists with God from the beginning – comes down from heaven as God's bride with her dowry of sacraments. With outstretched arms she offers the eucharist as a priest, gathering the faithful and the penitent with the healing fragrance of her sacrifice upon the fiery breast of her love (101).

For the mystics the Church is the bride who becomes one flesh with God in Christ. She is Christ on earth. Christ's sufferings are her labour pains (Jn 16:20-21), which she endures to bring her children to new birth in Christ (101; Gal 4:19). Like Mary, (118), she represents the pregnant hope and pain of all creation, fulfilled in new birth in the Spirit (33, 70; Rom 8:22-23). As Christ wants to embrace God's children in the outstretched arms of the cross, like a mother hen gathering her chicks (Mt 23:37), so the Church's vocation to motherhood (Mk 3:35; Gal 4:26; 2 Jn 1) is expressed in nursing the same children (1 Cor 3:2; 1 Thess 2:7) with the milk of the sacraments drawn from Christ's breast (86, 106, 113; Jn 19:34). She offers the Christ whose body she is.

From these insights it will be clear that the inclusive imagery and language which this book portrays are not a new liturgical trend but the rediscovery of the Church's Scripture and Tradition. Our task is not to suppress male images of God in favour of females ones, still less to un-sex the Word made flesh, but to explore all the riches of

God's nature. As our prayer is not only expressive but formative, we need the vision of the mystics to help our prayer to grow, reinterpreting the Majesty and Kingship of God in terms of the Lover who claims a unique loyalty, and reaching out for the Motherhood of God who enfolds us and nurtures us, but also moves creatively and powerfully within us. Only in this wholeness of perspective can we find wholeness of God's love for us, for all humanity, and all creation.

NOTES

[1] Bernard of Clairvaux, *Sermon* 83.3
[2] Beguine Spirituality, (ed.) F. Bowie, p. 70
[3] Bernard of Clairvaux, *Sermon* 74.6f
[4] Gertrude the Great, *LDP* II. 7
[5] *Heart of Compassion*, (ed.) A.M. Allchin; trans. S. Brock, London 1989, p. 9
[6] Mechthild of Magdeburg, *VLG*, II.8, III.15
[7] Wolfram, *Parzival* V. 239-240
[8] Anselm, *Prayer to St Paul* II. 397-9
[9] Aelred of Rievaulx, *Speculum Caritatis* II.18

Lives of the mystics

Hroswith (Roswitha) (c. 935-1000)

A nun at the Benedictine convent of Gandersheim, founded by the Saxon royalty for their daughters, giving their fellow nuns a status contrasting with contemporary female subservience. Provoked by the popular portrayal of scandalous women in Terence's classical plays, Hroswith wrote six plays allegorising female strength of character and various poems on the life of Christ and the saints. Prayers: 43, 125.

Hildegard of Bingen, Saint (1098-1179)

Born of a noble family at Bermersheim, she had waking visions of the 'living light' from the age of three. Educated by the anchoress Jutta of Sponheim and later by the monk Volmar at Disibodenberg's Benedictine abbey, she became head of its convent in 1136. In 1141 a vision of blinding light revealing the meaning of Scripture changed her life and caused her to write 'Scivias' (Know the ways) and the 'Book of Divine Works'. Fighting all objections to her vocation, she founded autonomous communities at Rupertsberg (1150) and Eibingen (1165). Here she practised the healing arts of medicine and music: as a 'feather on the breath of God', she composed a musical morality play and over seventy hymns. Her public preaching denounced clerical corruption and called the Church to repentance. Kings, popes and laity alike sought her uncompromising counsel.

Feast day: 17 September. Prayers: 31-2, 34-5, 39, 44-7, 49, 51-53, 65-69, 93, 101-2, 113, 117-8, 120-4.

Elisabeth of Schönau, Saint (1129-1164)

A Benedictine nun at Schönau's double monastery near the Taunus hills. The disturbing visions of her twenties became more ordered from Pentecost 1152, inspired by the liturgical calendar and often revealed in ecstasy during mass. Abbot Hildelin encouraged her to record her visions for her brother Egbert to edit. She gave practical advice on Christian life, though her attacks on corrupt leaders brought her their ridicule. She became superior of the nuns in 1157, enriching their devotion to the eucharist, the saints and the Blessed Virgin Mary – her guide in the visions.

Feast day: 18 June. Prayers: 48, 62, 92, 108, 121.

Mechtild of Hackeborn, Saint (1241-1299)

In 1248 Mechtild visited her sister, Gertrude of Hacke-born, who was abbess of Rossdorf convent in Saxony. She stayed, moving with the community to Helfta in 1258. Though a caring novice mistress, she was re-nowned as 'God's nightingale' for her training of the choir. She regarded music as the meeting-place of Christ's body, where each melody resounded from the believer's heart to the heart of God. Singing the Psalter was also her prayerful weapon against the convent's opponents. Clergy neglecting their studies were often in the prayers of this keen student!

Feast day: 19 November. Prayers: 60-1, 80, 124.

Gertrude the Great, Saint (1256-1302)

From the age of five, Gertrude was brought up (as an orphan?) at the Cistercian convent at Helfta. On 27 January 1281 she was converted by a vision of Christ promising to make her drunk with the river of divine pleasure. Her contemplative life recorded in her 'Herald of God's loving kindness' (1289), centres on the divine lover drawing us by the love of the Sacred Heart into a union with the Godhead – consummated in the eucharist, whose frequent reception Helfta encouraged. She received the stigmata inwardly and, though impatient of faults, was a profound spiritual director, as her 'Exercises' on living the sacramental life illustrate.

Feast day: 16 November. Prayers: 32-3, 35, 37-8, 40, 57-9, 68, 70-72, 77, 79-86, 88, 105-7, 112-13, 119.

Mechthild of Magdeburg, Saint (c. 1212-1282)

She received visitations of the Holy Spirit from the age of twelve. Around 1230 she left home for Magdeburg to join the Beguines. Here Heinrich of Halle encouraged her to become a Dominican tertiary and dictate her revelations in 'The flowing light of the Godhead'. The persecution caused by her attacking corrupt priests as 'goats' drove her to seek refuge at Helfta in 1270. Her faith in Christ's redemptive suffering and her prayer for the lost spring from her personal experience of God's universal love which she celebrates in the poetry of courtly love.

Feast day: 15 August or 8 October. Prayers: 31-4, 36-7, 50, 54-6, 72, 75-9, 84, 86-7, 91-8, 105, 109, 111, 114, 119.

Margaret Ebner (d. 1351)

A nun at the convent of Maria-Mödingen near Ulm, influenced by the preacher Johannes Tauler (c. 1300-1361). At the suggestion of Heinrich of Nördlingen, she wrote down the 'Revelations' of her mystical life. Her correspondence is the first collection of letters in German. She was associated with the 'Friends of God'. Prayers: 50, 91.

Elisabeth Staeglin (c. 1300-1360)

A Dominican nun at the convent of Thöss near Winterthur, associated with the 'Friends of God'. She flourished under the spiritual direction of Heinrich Seuse (Suso, c. 1295-1366), a disciple of Eckhart. Her philosophical enquiry and love of God brought great joy to Seuse, whose work she edited and translated. Prayer: 36.

Dorothea of Montau, Saint (1347-1394)

Brought up in Montau (Marienburg) on the Vistula, she married Albert, a swordsmith from Gdansk, and bore nine children. During twenty-five years of a difficult marriage, she was influenced by the example of Birgitta of Sweden (c. 1303-1373), and won over her aggressive husband to the faith. After he died, she became a recluse at nearby Marienwerder, where, for the last year of her life, she gave herself to devotion to the Blessed Sacrament and counselling pilgrims, the fruits of which appear in her 'Seven lilies".
Feast day: 30 October. Prayer: 110.

The Heart
of the Creator

The love of all

Love overflows into all
Glorious from ocean's depths beyond the farthest star,
Bounteous in loving all creation;
For to the King most High
Love has given her kiss of peace.

Hildegard of Bingen
SACR 16

The light of all

You are the transcendent sun, the highest peak of
   burning fire,
You are the clear waxing moon, the well of fathomless
   desire,
You are height beyond all reach, brightness beyond
   measure,
Wisdom beyond depth,
Compassion beyond restraint,
Strength beyond constraint,
Crown of all glory,
Yours is the praise and glory
From the humblest creature you have made!

Mechthild of Magdeburg
VLG 1.8

The maker of all

The fish will never drown within the tide,
The birds fall from the air on which they ride,

The flame will not corrode or blacken gold,
For fire burns it pure and clean,
Gives it a shining colour.
To all creatures God has granted
To live according to their nature.
How then could I deny my breath and bone?
In all things I submit to God alone,
Who is my father by nature,
Who is my brother by humanity,
Who is my bridegroom by love,
And from the outset I am all God's own.

Mechthild of Magdeburg
VLG I.44
adapted from Carol North Valhope's translation

The Mother of all

Praise the Trinity!
For she is the voice and life,
The mother of every creature in life!
She is the praise of the angel host,
The wonderful splendour of mysteries
Unknown to human minds!
She is the life in everything!

Hildegard of Bingen
SACR 17

Love that nurtures

Holy Trinity,
you are the source
from whom the living Godhead shines, all love and
    wisdom.

From you springs God's own powerfulness,
insight from your mutual oneness,
overflowing sweetness, love-kindling kindness,
all-embracing holiness, all-pervasive goodness:
yours is the praise, the honour and the glory,
yours is the power and vision of prayer,
yours the offering of thankfulness!

And you, O Love, God yourself,
loving bond of the Holy Trinity,
you lie down to take your rest and pleasure
among earth's children in awesome purity,
yet ablaze with the fire of your love,
like a rose of beauty gathered from among the thorns!

O Love! You only know the paths of truth and living,
in you the Holy Trinity makes covenants of loving,
through you the Spirit's better gifts are working,
from you the seeds that suckle life's fruits are
    abounding,
from you the sweeter honey of God's joy is flowing,
from you the Lord of hosts pours richer drops of
    blessing,
the loving promise of the Spirit's treasure,
– rare beyond all measure!

Gertrude the Great
ESSIII
A prayer on the *Te Deum* for the anniversary of
a nun's profession

From the Father's heart

Lord Jesus Christ,
you flowed without beginning
from the heart of the eternal Father in the Spirit,

and were born of a pure, perfect virgin, Holy Mary,
in the flesh!
With your Father you are one spirit, one will, one
    wisdom,
one force, one supreme power over all that ever was
without end!

Lord, eternal Father,
though unworthy,
I also flowed from your heart in the spirit,
and, Lord Jesus Christ, from your wounded side
I was born in the flesh.
You are Lord, truly human and truly God,
and with your two-fold spirit I have been cleansed.
And so, in my poor plight I pray:
Lord, heavenly Father, you are my heart!
Lord, Jesus Christ, you are my body!
Lord, Holy Spirit, you are my breath!
Lord, Holy Trinity,
you are my only refuge and my eternal rest!

Mechthild of Magdeburg
VLG V.6

The miracle of human life

How wonderful is the foreknowledge of God's heart,
Who knew every creature before we ever came to be!
For God gazed upon the human face
And saw that all creation
Came to perfection in the human form.
How wonderful is the Breath of God
Who brought human beings such life!

Hildegard of Bingen
SACR 60
cf Gen 2:7

Treasured by God

O the dignity of that small speck of human dust,
taken by the jewel of heavenly excellence
to raise us from the clay of earth to heaven's height!
O the excellence of that frail flower,
drawn from marshy ground
by the sun's own ray
to make her shine in splendour with God!
O the happiness of that blessed soul
whom the Lord of majesty treasures with such dignity!
We are as far removed
as a creature can be from her Creator,
yet God has made the soul
in the beauty of the divine image!

Gertrude the Great
LDP II.9

Enfolded in God

O Power of Wisdom,
In your encompassing
You have encompassed all that has life,
Enfolding all things in one course
With your three wings:
One soars up to heaven's height,
Another skims the earth, dripping with dew in flight,
A third moves everywhere from depth to height.
Praise to you, as is your due, O Wisdom!

Hildegard of Bingen
SACR 59
cf Sir 24:5-6

Safe in God

I pray, Lord, that you may come to me
As a faithful father to a dear child,
And protect for me the goal of my pilgrim path.
With my sinful mouth there is nothing I can say,
So come and speak to my soul within,
Comfort her and always keep her safe,
That I may be filled with joy, and not despair.
Grant this, Lord, for your loving kindness' sake.

Mechthild of Magdeburg
VLG VII.35
Prayers on the seven penitential psalms: Ps 102(101)

Uplifted in God

Praise God!
I have been shown, as far as can be,
what God is and where God is...

Wonder of all!
I swim in the Godhead
like an eagle in the air.

Elisabeth Staeglin of Thöss
VHS LI
cf Deut 32:11-12

The ways of God

We praise you, Lord, that you have searched for us
 with humbleness,
We praise you, Lord, that you have cared for us with
 tenderness,

We praise you, Lord, that you have adorned us with
   lowliness,
We praise you, Lord, that you have guided us with
   gentleness,
We praise you, Lord, that you have ruled us with
   wiseness,
We praise you, Lord, that you have guarded us with
   powerfulness,
We praise you, Lord, that you have hallowed us with
   greatness,
We praise you, Lord, that you have counselled us with
   trustfulness,
We praise you, Lord, that you have lifted us to new
   heights with your love.

Mechthild of Magdeburg
VLG I.6

My love, my God, my joy

I will praise you, my God and King!
My King and my God, my love, my God, my joy,
My heart and soul rejoice in you!
Life of my soul, my living, true God,
fount of eternal light,
light whose refreshing face is imprinted on my
   unworthiness,
my heart longs to welcome you and praise you,
to tell of your greatness and bless you!
I give you the core of all my powers and feelings,
an offering full of fresh praises and deepest
   thanksgiving.

And how may I repay you, my Lord,
for all your good gifts to me?
For I can see that you have loved me
above your own glory:
you did not spare yourself for me;
you created me for yourself;
you redeemed me and chose me for yourself
to draw me to yourself and let me live in you
and enjoy you in happiness for ever.
For what have I in heaven apart from you?
What can I want beyond all your good gifts except
    you?

My Lord, you are my hope,
you are my glory, my joy, my happiness,
you are the thirst of my spirit, the life of my soul,
the joy of my heart!
Where shall my praise lead but to you, O God?
You are the beginning and end of all goodness,
you are the home of all who share your joy,
you are the praise of my heart and mouth!
You shine like the dawn and blossom like the spring
in the pleasure of your joyful love.
May the power of your Godhead bring you praise and
    glory,
for you are the source of eternal light and the fount of
    life!

Gertrude the Great
ESS VI
A meditation on praise and thanksgiving
inspired by Ps 145 (144)

Mother of justice

'I have been brought by my Sovereign Love
into the royal chambers.
We shall be glad and rejoice in you,
as we think of your breasts,
more nourishing than wine.
Those who live justly love you.'

With our whole body and soul
all of us redeemed by the blood of God's Son
are glad and rejoice in you, O Holy Godhead!
Through you we have our being,
and we recall the sweetness of our heavenly reward
more than all the sufferings and trials
that we have suffered from truth's enemies.
All that we count as nothing,
while we taste the delights you offer us
in the revelation of your commandments.
And so those who show justice by their holy deeds
love you with a true and perfect love,
because you give all good things to those who love
    you,
and, in the end, you even grant them eternal life.

But for the chambers of the human mind
Wisdom also pours and serves the justice of true faith,
through which the true God is known.
Therefore, the faithful thirst for God's justice,
and they suck holiness from her breasts,
never to be wearied, while they are being refreshed
contemplating the Godhead,
for holiness surpasses all human understanding!

Hildegard of Bingen
LDO I. Vision II.19
cf Song of Songs 1:4; Phil 3:8; Rom 8:28; Mt 5:6

Wisdom of all

O wonderful Wisdom of God,
how strong, how clear is your voice!
You call to yourself all who desire you,
and make no exception.
You live in the humble,
you love those who love you,
you give justice for the cause of the poor,
you are faithful, showing mercy to all,
you hate nothing that you have made,
you make our human sins appear as nothing,
and, with tender heart,
you look to us to repent...

O Wisdom, all things go well with you!
You are the only one who can do all things.
You stay constant within yourself,
yet you make all things new...

How wisely you encompass all things!
How carefully you planned our salvation!
You embraced the King of glory,
revealed the plan of peace,
fulfilling the demands of God's love and power,
and seized the moment for love
to carry on the cross the people' sin.
O Wisdom of God,
no evil could hinder your wonderful works,
no human folly change your faithful purpose,
no sin blot out that great love and goodness,
for your royal work prevailed in power,
to bring all things to a sweet end.

Gertrude the Great
ESS VII
Preparation for one's own death

40

The Heart of the
Saviour

The Saviour's birth

Praise above all praises is your due, O Christ of glory,
Wonderful the power which constantly fulfils your
   purpose!
Silently you make the smallest move and change
   creation!
Who can dare desire the gifts of such great loving
   kindness?
Only Son of God, true likeness of the Father's nature,
Who dare gaze on you or praise your wondrous deeds
   to save us?

Though begotten of the Father's love without
   beginning,
You obeyed God's will and filled the womb of Holy
   Mary,
Taking human form from her with all time's passing
   limits.
You can hold the whole world in the palm of your
   great power,
Yet you let yourself be bound in common baby
   clothing!
Though you dwell beyond the skies on starry plains of
   heaven,
There you lay within a cave, constricted in a manger!
You alone can name the galaxies of constellations,
Number every raindrop, every sandy shore of ocean,
But so patiently you sucked the breasts of Mother
   Mary.

Fearlessly in faithful trust you fled King Herod's
   vengeance,
Showing all the world the real path of human living.
Soon you softened stony hearts of unbelieving pagans,

Making nations feel your firm and righteous rule for
  ever,
So that, taught by holy sacraments, they came to know
  you
As the One who by your word alone created all
  things,
Jesus Christ, proclaimed by oracles of all the prophets.

Therefore, to your Father now and through the length
  of ages
Let all creatures give the glory and eternal praises,
For God's love for us would not spare you, the
  Beloved;
And to you, O Christ, be everlasting power and
  triumph,
For you shed your blood to save a world about to
  perish;
Everlasting praise to you and to the Holy Spirit,
Through whom every heavenly gift and grace are
  poured upon us!

Hroswith (Roswitha) of Gandersheim
Pl. Epilogue

The Word made flesh

O Strength of all eternity,
In your heart you have ordered all things:
Through your Word
All things have been created,
As you willed.
And this very Word of yours
Was clothed in flesh
In the same form which sprang from Adam.
And so that human clothing has been cleansed

44

From its greatest grief and pain.
How great is the kindness of the Saviour
Who has set all things free
By taking our flesh –
A wonder which God's power breathed forth
Without the shackles of sin!

Hildegard of Bingen
SACR 58
cf Jn 1

The refugee

Lord God almighty,
King of kings and Lord of lords,
you sit enthroned upon the cherubim,
everything in heaven, on earth and in the depths
kneels before you!
Yet you were ready to take flight in human flesh
from the persecution of an earthly king into Egypt,
that, in every part of life,
you might show us an example of humility,
and come to know our fragile human nature,
made of dust and clay.
You have met every failing of our soul's sickness
with the various medicines of your saving health.
Whatever misfortune may befall us,
we may take comfort from the faith and mercy
which you showed in your distress.

Therefore, my Redeemer and my Lord,
be my refuge in my sin and poverty,
in my flight call me back home to you,
for I have often hurt you with my many failings.
Hold me as I flee!
Support me with your help
to escape all the ambushes of my enemies, seen and
    unseen.

By the power of your Name
make me travel through every danger and distress
each day I call to you in prayer.

Hildegard of Bingen
GB XVIII
cf Mt 2:13-15

The baptism of Christ

O faithful Lord Jesus Christ,
only begotten Son of the living God,
Creator and redeemer of the human race!
You showed the proof of the Father's love
in the flesh of humanity.
It was your will to be baptised in water by Saint John,
as the Holy Spirit descended in the form of a dove,
and so, you made all water holy by your baptism.
To wash away the dirt of sin from every believer
you give us grace to see in these waters
the great mystery of your faithfulness,
by which sinners may go down into the font
and rise up purified.
They go down a child of death,
they rise up a child of resurrection;
they go down a child of strife,
they rise up a child of reconciliation;
they go down a child of wrath,
they rise up a child of tender heart;
they go down a child of the devil,
they rise up a child of God!

These are the gifts of your mercy, most merciful God,
which you have granted us by your baptism,
for you alone have no sin.
Therefore, O most tender-hearted Christ,
cleanse me from all wrongdoing in body and soul,

and mercifully forgive all the sin I have done
since my baptism,
that I may receive eternal life, my Saviour.
You live and reign in the Trinity throughout the ages
of ages!

Hildegard of Bingen
GB XX
cf Mt 3:16-17

The wedding

O heavenly Bridegroom,
Lord Jesus Christ,
you came down from heaven to earth
to be betrothed to your human bride.
For, though the Son of God,
you came as the Son of Man to a wedding,
to show a mystery of spiritual grace by your miracle.
You changed this water into wine,
wonderfully converting the antiquity of the old law
into the sweetness of the Gospel,
which proclaims the forgiveness of sins.

Make me change from sin to goodness;
Let me not stay in this tasteless way of life,
but let the wine of heavenly grace
make the dry heart of my soul drunk.
Help me to show true repentance and continue in
good works,
that I may never be separated
from the marriage of your bride, the Church.

Hildegard of Bingen
GB XXIII
cf Jn 2:1-11

The name of Jesus

O Lord Jesus,
Jesus – the good name, the precious name,
the name which is above every name,
the name that no one can know
unless they accept it,
the name that no one can speak
unless spoken in the Holy Spirit.
Sweet and pleasant name,
wonderful and loveable,
strong and saving name of Jesus!
Jesus – the name that is faithful and joyful,
the name of good hope that comforts the sinner!
For what is 'JESUS' if not 'the Saviour'?

Therefore, Jesus,
for your own sake
be for me my Jesus.
Good Jesus, kind Jesus,
for your name's sake deal with me according to your
     name.
You created me so that I might not perish:
be for me my Jesus.
You redeemed me so that I might not perish:
be for me my Jesus.

Elisabeth of Schönau
GB XIV
cf Phil 2:9; 1 Cor 12:3

The light of the blind

O Light and Guide of the blind,
you enlighten everyone coming into this world!
For you opened the eyes of the man born blind
with paste which you made from the spittle of your
    own mouth.

By this miracle you have shown us
that the Word became flesh.
The human race, blind from the beginning,
received eternal light
through your earthly life in the flesh
which you took for us.
You became the dust of the earth for us,
yet, by the power of your majesty,
you enlightened our darkness.
As you brought healing by the earthly paste of your
    spittle,
so, the Word made flesh for us gives us the greatest
    hope
that the murky night of darkness will not overwhelm
    us,
but we shall see the daylight of eternity.

Lord, let us receive your clear light;
be for us such a mirror of light
that we may be given grace to see you unendingly.
If we are overcome, you have the power to forgive us:
therefore, in my sin I call on you, my Light, for help,
for you were sent into the world
to enlighten my heart, to nurture true repentance,
and to make the Holy Spirit's work grow powerfully in
    me.
With the Father and the Holy Spirit
you live and reign for ever!

Hildegard of Bingen
GB XLIII
cf Jn 9

The joy of Jesus

O sweet Jesus,
loveliest form of all,
you do not hide from the need or love of my poor
    soul,
and with that soul I praise you,
in love, in need,
in loving fellowship with all your creatures.
This is my delight above all else!

Lord,

> you are the sun of every eye,
> you are the delight of every ear,
> you are the sound of every word,
> you are the power of every skill,
> you are the teaching of every wisdom,
> you are the love of every life,
> you are the order of every being!

Mechthild of Magdeburg
VLG III.2

Jesus the teacher

Jesus Christ, you are my dearest love,
    have mercy on me.
Jesus Christ, you are pure truth,
    teach me truth.
Jesus Christ, you are sweet love,
    teach me love.
Jesus Christ, you are inexhaustible compassion,
    come to my help.

Margaret Ebner
Off. 67a

Mary of Magdala

Holy Mary of Magdala,
you came with a fount of tears
to the Fount of tenderheartedness,
whose glow of overwhelming warmth you felt,
bringing you back from sin to life,
as you found sweet comfort in your bitter pain.
Dear Mary, you have proved yourself
that a sinner may be reconciled to her Creator.
May Christ's loving purpose have mercy on me;
may that same medicine restore my listless soul to
    health.
You were the Lord's dear love and you knew well that
    love,
forgiving you your many sins,
because you loved so much!

I am not the worst sinner, blessed Mary,
but I long with hope for that mercy
by which our sins are blotted out.
I am unhappy and plunged into the depths of sin,
weighed down with the burden,
imprisoned in shadows, cut off from myself,
cloaked in darkness.
I have been chosen and loved,
loved by God's own choice,
yet I am unhappy and seek your help, blessed Mary,
for you have made the darkness light.

Hildegard of Bingen
GB XLIX
cf Lk 7:36-8:3

A woman healed

O saving Health of the world and eternal Life,
for our life and health you came down from heaven!
You took our flesh upon you and became a human
    being,
while you were truly God of heaven,
so that you might bring lost humanity
back home to heaven.
For, though the cherubim and seraphim fear to look
    on you
in the almighty power of your heavenly majesty,
you let a poor woman touch the fringe of your
    garment
when you wore your earthly body!
And so, at once she received her health again,
for she had found the true fount of tender-
    heartedness.

Now, Lord, with that same tender heart,
stem the flow of my soul's sins,
which I have suffered every day of my life.
As I shed the tears of true repentance,
may I receive the perfect recovery of my health.
O Jesus, lover of humanity, saviour of the world,
you have atoned for every sin
without fear of condemnation in your paradise:
let me be one with you for ever
through your holy and glorious Name,
God, three in one;
for you live and reign throughout all ages of ages!

Hildegard of Bingen
GB XXVIII
cf Lk 8:43-48

A woman forgiven

How wonderful is your kindness, O God,
how amazing your tenderheartedness,
revered by the angels in heaven!
Sinners find trust to seek you in every need and
    trouble,
and implore your tender heart.
For you came down from the Mount of Olives
to the temple where they presented to you
the woman taken in adultery
who had despised the holy law.
You came from the highest mount of heaven to earth,
full of the oil of gladness
and generous forgiveness for sinners.
This was how you met this solitary woman caught in
    her sin,
for neither now nor ever
will you cease to welcome sinners!

Though unworthy, we are filled with hope in you,
when we hear that, after her last accuser left,
these two remained: the wretched heart and the tender
    heart.
And so the wretched woman could not be
    condemned,
for Christ remained with tender heart.

By that same tender heart,
God of mercy,
do not condemn me in my wretchedness.

Hildegard of Bingen
GB XXIX
cf Jn 8:1-11

The fruit of the cross

O heavy dew of God's great being,
O tender flower of the sweet Virgin,
O vital fruit of that fair flower,
O holy offering of the heavenly Father,
O faithful pledge redeeming all the world!

Take my morning prayer of praise!
Let my praise resound with the glory
Of your wretched birth, your wretched need,
Your cruel passion and your holy death,
Your glorious resurrection and your beautiful
    ascension,
And all for the glory of your almighty glory!

Remember me, dear Lord;
In all my doing and my self-denying,
In all my daily living,
Help me to carry through your holy will,
That good may come for the glory of your holy
    Trinity.
This I pray for all who are with me,
Who, in your name, are your friends and mine.

Mechthild of Magdeburg
VLG VII.18
for Matins, from the Office of the Passion

The burden of the cross

O heavy burden,
O wretched weight that we are, Lord,
Yet you have carried us with your cross!

Carry us, Lord, beyond all our strife
Into eternal life.

O bloody strife,
O wounds so deep, O pain so great!
Let me not perish, Lord,
In all my tortured strife.

O most blessed strife,
O most holy death,
O most wondrous mirror of the Father's love,
Jesus Christ,
High on the cross, nailed hand and foot!
I commend my soul to you, Lord, at my last end,
That I may be inseparably one with you for ever,
As your heavenly Father was and is with you.
Grant this prayer for me
And for all who truly love you.

Mechthild of Magdeburg
VLG VII.18
for Terce, Sext and None from the Office of the Passion

The wounded heart

O love bound to the cross, yet flowing free!
O heart, true and steadfast, pouring forth!
O body of noble life, killed for me!
My dearest love, Jesus Christ!

Hear my prayer:
May my five senses have the grace
To find unceasing joy
In the bloody spear
And the wounds of your sweet heart.

May my poor soul have the grace
To find that eternal joy within me
Together with those who are with me,
For whom, in Christian love, I ought and want to pray.

Mechthild of Magdeburg
VLG VII.18
for Vespers from the Office of the Passion
Cf Jn 19:34-37

The love of the crucified

O deepest and holiest of all humility!
O broadest and most gracious of all gifts!
O highest and most glorious love,
Love of all love, Jesus Christ,
Love in which you pray to your heavenly Father!
Fulfil now, Lord, your prayer for us:
Make us holy in the truth,
And give us the depth of all humility
That we may want to serve all creatures,
For creatures resist those who do not do so.
Give us, Lord, the breadth of all graciousness,
Freely fulfilling everything in our daily duties
Through your love.
And give us, Lord, your love of such a height
To keep us pure in you
And uncorrupted by all earthly things.

Mechthild of Magdeburg
VLG VII.18
for Compline from the Office of the Passion
cf Jn 17:17; Eph 3:17-19

Heart speaks to heart

Most tenderhearted Lord,
inscribe your wounds on my heart
with your precious blood.
Let me read in them your suffering
equalled only by your love.
Let the thought of your wounds
constantly stay in the secret place of my heart.
Let the pain of your compassion be aroused within
    me,
and the fire of your love kindled within me.

Gertrude the Great
LDP II.4
A prayer on the gift of the stigmata

The wound of love

By your pierced heart,
most loving Lord,
transfix the heart of your love
so deeply with its darts
that it may hold within it nothing earthly
that is not held by the power of your Godhead alone.

Gertrude the Great
LDP II.5

Signed with the cross

In the name of the Father,
and of the Son,
and of the Holy Spirit.

From you, my crucified love, sweet Jesus,
let me receive the sign of your holy cross
in my heart as on my forehead,
that I may live for ever under your protection.
Give me the living faith of heavenly teaching
that I may run the way of your commandments
with a ready heart.
Through you may I live in such a way
that I may worthily become the temple of God
and the home of the Holy Spirit.

Gertrude the Great
ESS I
A meditation on baptism
cf 1 Cor 3:16

Living water

Come, Jesus, fountain of life,
let me drink of your living water,
that, when I have once tasted you,
I may thirst for nothing in eternity but you.
Plunge me wholly into the deep waters of your
   tenderheartedness
Baptise me in the spotless purity of your precious
   death.
Renew me by the blood through which you have
   redeemed me.
In the water from your wounded side
wash away every spot of sin
by which I have ever stained the innocence of my
   baptism.
Fill me again with your Spirit,
and keep me wholly yours in purity of body
   and soul.

Gertrude the Great
ESS I
A meditation on baptism

Carrying the cross

Jesus,
by the love of your love,
make me always bear the easy yoke of your
    commandments
and carry this light burden on my shoulders;
let me wear this sign of faith on my breast for ever,
like a garland of holy myrrh,
that you may remain my Jesus,
crucified for me,
always fixed in my heart.

Gertrude the Great
ESS I
A meditation on baptism;
cf Mt 11:29-30

The light of Christ

Come, Jesus, my inextinguishable Light,
light the lamp of your love
and let it burn within me with inextinguishable flame;
teach me how to keep my baptism beyond reproach,
that, when I am called to come to your marriage-feast,
I may be ready and worthy to enter into the joys of
    eternal life,
when I shall see you, the true Light,
and gaze upon the refreshing face of your Godhead.

Gertrude the Great
ESS I
A meditation on baptism

Easter glory

I praise you and adore you,
I worship your greatness and your glory,
and I bless you, good Jesus!
Beyond all telling was your joy,
when your blest humanity was glorified
by the Father of divine glory
at your resurrection.
Then with divine power the Father gave eternal glory
to all who have been chosen
to share the life of God.

By that joy beyond all telling, I pray:
Loving mediator between humanity and God,
by your grace, keep bright and clear that same hope
which you won for me by your resurrection,
that I may claim its promise with joy
at the day of judgement.

Mechtild of Hackeborn
LSG I.19

Easter joy

I praise you and adore you,
I worship your greatness and your glory,
and I bless you, good Jesus!
Beyond all telling was your joy
when that priceless love
which brought you from the Father's breast into the
    world
and made you share all its pain and sorrow,
filled all your limbs again with incomparable joy and
    honour
at your resurrection,

as the Father had filled them with intolerable suffering
on the cross.

By that joy beyond all telling, I pray:
Loving mediator between humanity and God,
give me the light of understanding
and the knowledge of my soul,
that I may know at all times
what is acceptable to you.

Mechtild of Hackeborn
LSG I.19

Easter victory

I praise you and adore you,
I worship your greatness and your glory,
and I bless you, good Jesus!
Beyond all telling was your joy,
when God the Father gave you full authority
to show the greatness of your generosity
and recompense, enrich and honour
all your friends and fellow soldiers
whom you freed from the tyrant's power
and led forth in your glorious victory procession.

By that joy beyond all telling, I pray:
Loving mediator between humanity and God,
make me share all your works and struggles;
make me share your glorious death and blessed
    passion.

Mechtild of Hackeborn
LSG I.19

I adore you

Lord Jesus Christ, I adore you;
you ascended on the cross
and bore the crown of thorns on your brow:
may this same cross free me from the power of death.
I adore you, wounded on the cross,
drunk with gall and vinegar:
may your wounds be the medicine for my soul.
I adore you, buried in the tomb:
let your death be my life.
I adore you, for you descended into hell and freed the
    captives:
do not let me enter hell.
I adore you, for you ascended into heaven,
and you sit at the right hand of the Father:
look upon me in your mercy.
I adore you, for you will come in judgement
to judge the living and the dead:
at your coming,
do not enter into judgement with me, a sinner,
but let me seek your mercy,
and ask you to forgive my past sins,
when you come to judge in judgement.

Elisabeth of Schönau
GB XVII

The fire of love

The fire of love

O Fire of the Spirit,
Comforter and advocate,
Life of the life of all creation,
You are holy in giving each form life.

You are holy in anointing the perilously broken,
You are holy in dressing the septic wound.

O Breath of holiness, Fire of charity,
Sweet taste in the breast and cordial of the heart,
How good is the fragrance of your powers!

O Fount of clearest water,
In whom we see God gathering the strangers and
    seeking the lost!

O Breastplate of life,
Hope of unity for all Christ's members,
Belt of truth and honesty:
Save your chosen people!

Keep safe those who have been imprisoned by the
    enemy,
And release the fettered,
For it is God's will and power to save them.

O bold Path, penetrating all creation,
In the heights, on the earth, and in the deepest
    places,
You gather and bind all people together!

From you the clouds fly, the air flows,
The stones have their moisture,
The waters draw forth their brooks,
And the earth exudes her green freshness.

You are also continually nurturing the learned,
Making them glad with the inspiration of your
   wisdom.

Therefore, all praise is yours,
For you are the voice of praise and the joy of life,
Our hope and highest honour, offering the prize of
   light!

Hildegard of Bingen
SACR 19

Spirit of life

Holy Spirit,
You are life-giving life,
The moving force of everything,
And the root of all creation.
You cleanse everything
From the stain on its earthly beauty,
Wiping away sins
And anointing wounds.
In all these ways your life shines forth,
Wakening and re-awakening everything to life:
You are worthy of all praise!

Hildegard of Bingen
SACR 15

Spirit of burning

O Spirit of burning,
Yours is the praise,
Celebrated in the music of strings and drums!

Human minds catch fire from you,
And the homes of our souls sustain their strength from
    you.
From you the will ascends and gives the soul a
    foretaste,
And desire is her guiding light.
Our understanding calls on your help with sweetest
    sound,
And with all our powers of reasoning
Prepares for you a temple, exuding in works of gold.

When the spirit stirs
To try to see the eye of evil and the face of
    wickedness,
You purge it swiftly in your fire,
As and when you will.
But when our reasoning lies low through evil deeds,
You wound and break it as you will,
And restore it
Through the medicine of experience.

Therefore all creatures praise you,
For they have their life from you.
You are the most precious ointment
For broken and septic wounds,
Which you change into the most precious jewels.

Now make it your pleasure
To gather us all to yourself,
And guide us on the right paths.

Hildegard of Bingen
SACR 18

The refiner's fire

O glowing Fire that makes us lonely without you,
you kindle your living flame, my God,
and brand me!
With inextinguishable blaze
you burn powerfully in the dampness of my fickle
    soul.
First you dry the flow of earthly pleasure in her,
and then you soften the numbness of her feelings.

O all-consuming Fire,
you bring your power to bear upon our sins,
that you may gently show us
how your anointing changes us.
From you alone we receive the grace
to be remoulded into our Maker's likeness.

O forge of God's power,
revealing your welcome vision of true peace!
By your working, our dross is turned to gold,
tried and chosen.
Weary at last with deceit,
the soul is kindled with longing
to seek with all her will's desire
the gift which is hers to have
from you, her real Truth!

Gertrude the Great
LDP II.7
cf 1 Pet 1:6-7

The Fire of Pentecost

O Giver of constant consolation,
Jesus Christ, Saviour of the world!
You sent your faithful followers
the Holy Spirit, the Comforter,

with tongues of fire from heaven:
you wanted them to show the faith of the Holy Trinity
clearly to all the nations
in all their varied languages throughout the world!
For the Holy Spirit is an artist of creative power,
and works the change of God's grace,
making a shepherd a royal psalmist,
a fisherman and tax-collector evangelists,
a persecutor a great preacher and teacher of the
    nations;
and many sinners today are changed
by the same creative and comforting Spirit
from the dirt of sin to cleanness.

How good is this Physician, Jesus,
whom you have sent to all the members of your body
who believe in you!
Let them be restored to health by the medicines
which the Spirit, the Comforter, draws from you
and offers us for the world.
And cleanse me, Lord, from my sins' sickness,
root out its roots utterly from me:
pride, boasting, greed, hatred, envy,
extravagance, lying and sullenness.
Do not let my Guest, the Holy Spirit, spurn my heart's
    home,
but be ready to make a dwelling-place in me.
I make this prayer through you,
Jesus Christ, Saviour of the world:
you live and reign, God, to the ages of ages. Amen.

Hildegard of Bingen
GB LXXI
cf Acts 2

A new birth

Holy Father,
through your Son, our Lord Jesus Christ,
you have given me a new birth
by water and the Holy Spirit:
forgive me fully all my sins today
and anoint me with the oil of your Spirit
for eternal life.

Gertrude the Great
ESS I
A meditation of baptism
Cf Jn 3:5

A new heart

My dear delight, my God, my heart of tenderness!
Come now and send your Holy Spirit from above,
and create in me a new heart and a new spirit.
Come with your anointing and teach me all things,
for I have chosen you before a thousand others,
and I love you more dearly than every love,
even the love of my own soul.
Let my soul grow in grace and power,
as full of the glory and beauty of love
as you will,
for I long for you with all my heart.

Gertrude the Great
ESS IV
A meditation on religious profession
cf Ps 51(50):10; Ez 36:26-27; Jn 14:26

A new family

Lord God,
when you created me,
you made me so that you could change me.
Bring your Holy Spirit anew into my heart,
add me to the people you have adopted as your own,
and fill me with the joy that you have accepted me
among the children of your promise –
a joy I have, not by my own nature, but by your grace.

Make me strong in faith,
        joyful in hope,
        patient in trouble,
        happy to praise you,
        on fire with the Spirit,
        faithful to serve you,
        Lord God, my true king,
        and persevering to watch with you
        till the end of my life.

Gertrude the Great
ESS I
A meditation on confirmation;
cf Rom 12:11-13

Living in the Spirit

Lord,
through the gift of your Spirit,
make me skilful in discretion,
wise in kindness,
strong in gentleness,
pure in freedom.

Let me burn with charity,
let me love nothing apart from you,
let me live a praiseworthy life,
yet not seek to be praised.
Let me give you glory
in holiness of body and purity of spirit.
Let me choose to love you with love
and serve you with love.
I want you to be my reward,
you to be my joy and pleasure,
my comfort in sorrow, my guidance in uncertainty.
You will be my defence, when I am hurt,
my patience, when I am troubled,
my wealth, when I am poor,
my food, when I am hungry,
my sleep, when I have to keep awake,
my medicine, when I am sick.

Gertrude the Great
ESS III
A prayer for the anniversary of a nun's profession

Lover and beloved

The lover and the beloved

God: I come to my beloved
         As the dew to the flower.

The soul: What joyful vision! What lovely greeting!
         What rapturous embrace!
         Lord! Your wonders have wounded me,
         Your mercy has mowed me down.
         O towering rock, so well and firmly wrought
         That none may rest in you
         Save dove and nightingale!

God: Welcome, sweet dove,
         You flew so high on earth
         That your wings are grown
         In the kingdom of heaven,
         Your savour is that of grapes,
         Your scent is that of balsam,
         Your radiance is like the sun,
         You are the waxing of my highest love.

The soul: O God who gushes gifts!
         O God who laves with love!
         O God who sears with desire!
         O God who melts in the fusion of the body!
         O God who rests in my breast,
         I cannot breathe without you!

God: O beautiful rose among thorns!
         O bee that flew to the honey!
         O dove whose day is serene!
         O sun with beautiful sheen!
         O moon in the fullness of light!
         I cannot turn from you.

You are my bed,
My most secret rest,
My want that grew and grew,
My highest honour.
You are the joy of my Godhead,
The solace of my humanity,
A river for my blaze.

Mechthild of Magdeburg
VLG I.12-20
cf Song of Songs 2:1.14, 5:1, 6:10
adapted from Carol North Valhope's translation

The lovers' dance

I cannot dance, Lord, unless you take me away with
    you!
If you want me to spring into step,
You must lead the song!
Then I shall dance my way into love,
From love into discovery,
From discovery into pleasure,
From pleasure beyond all human experience.
There I will stay,
And yet move forward in the circle of the dance.

Mechthild of Magdeburg
VLG I.44
cf Dante, *Paradise* xxiv.10-18

Lovers' praise

God praises the bride:

> You are a light unrivalled anywhere,
> You are a crowning garland of maidens fair,
> You are for every wound a perfect cure,
> You are among false friends true and sure,
> You are a bride of the Holy Trinity.

The bride praises God:

> You are in every light a light most pure,
> You are for every garland a flower mature,
> You are for every wound a perfect cure,
> You are unchangeably true, with no false deceit,
> You are a host to make each home secure.

> *Mechthild of Magdeburg*
> *VLG II.9-10*

Who is like you?

Who is like you, my Lord Jesus Christ,
my sweet love?
You are boundless in might and majesty,
and yet you care for the humble.
Who can compare with you in power, Lord?
Yet you choose the weak of the world.
Who can be as gracious as you are?
You laid the foundations of heaven and earth,
and their thrones and powers worship you,
and yet you seek your pleasure with human beings.

How great you are,
King of kings and Lord of lords!
You command the stars,

77

yet you set your heart upon human beings.
How gracious you are!
Riches and glory are in your hand,
you have your fill of every pleasure,
yet you choose to have a bride from earth.
O Love, for whom do you demean your majesty?
Come, my Love,
for whom do you channel the fount of your wisdom?
– For the depths of wretchedness.
O Love, yours alone,
yours alone is this excellent, abundant wine,
by which my heart is bound and drunk!

Gertrude the Great
ESS III
A meditation for the anniversary of a nun's profession

You are mine

Welcome, my living God!
You are mine above all else.
This is my endless joy,
That I may speak with you without pretence.
When my enemies hunt me down,
I flee into your arms,
Where I can pour out my troubles
And know that you will turn to me.
You know how well you can touch my soul
And make music on her strings:
Begin with me now, Lord,
And be happy for evermore.
True, I am an unworthy bride,
But you are my worthy bridegroom,
And so I shall enjoy you for ever.
Remember, Lord, how you can woo the pure soul

78

In your embrace,
And fulfil your love in me here and now,
For I am your first and only love.
Come then, Lord, draw me to yourself,
And I shall be pure and bright;
For if you leave me to myself,
I shall stay in pain and darkness.

Mechthild of Magdeburg
VLG V.17

Caressing

Come, kind Father, God of heaven above,
Draw my soul, all flowing and untroubled round your
    love,
And flow towards me, Lord,
With all the joy that is within you.
So let me give myself in prayer
And praise you to the full for all your good to me.
Come then, give me, Lord, your own threefold caress
In the sweet course of true love's gentleness,
That I may worthily enjoy the graciousness
Of all your kind gifts,
And may I never ask of you, sweet Lord,
Anything that is not for your praise.

Mechthild of Magdeburg
VLG V.35

Embracing

Come, Jesus, bridegroom of beauty,
let your love transpose my heart to you,
as death transposes soul from body.
Let me cleave to you with the indissoluble seal of love!

Take me, my Jesus, into the ocean of your tender-
    heartedness;
wash me clean of every stain in the depths of your
    mercy;
take me, my Jesus, into the embrace of your loving,
and let me become one with you
in a covenant of perfect union.
Take me, my Jesus, into your love's sweet
    consummation;
there let me enjoy the kiss of your honeyed lips.

Gertrude the Great
ESS III
A prayer for the anniversary of a nun's profession

Offering the heart

I praise you and I bless you,
I give you glory and I welcome you,
Jesus Christ, sweetest, kindest heart,
my faithful Lover.
Thank you for your safe keeping
with which you have protected me this night
and endlessly paid for me every debt of praise and
    thanks
I owed the Father.
And now, my only Lover,
I offer you my heart as a rose in full bloom
whose loveliness shall charm your gaze all day
and whose fragrance shall delight your heart of God.
I offer you my heart, too, as a cup of wine
from which you may drink your own sweetness
in everything you do through me today.
Above all, I offer you my heart as a fruit of the finest
    taste
fit for your royal banquet;

consume it and draw it into yourself
that it may feel happy within you.
And I pray that my every thought and word, deed and
    will,
may be guided today to please your gracious will.

Mechtild of Hackeborn
LSG III.17

I am yours

God of my life,
what praises can I offer you,
what can I give you, my Beloved,
for all the good things you have given me?
Therefore, for my sacrifice of praise, dearest Jesus,
I offer you in me and me in you:
it is all I have.
This life I have and live in you –
this I give you wholly.

You are my life, you are all I need, you are my glory!
You are the proof of God's tender heart
shining in my soul.
All praise and thanks are yours!
When shall I give the depths of my soul
to the flames of your altar,
kindling my heart with that ever-burning holy fire,
and offer you my whole being as a sacrifice of praise?

Come, my God, sweet and holy,
open my heart and make my soul grow within you,
that, deep within, all my being may be filled with your
    glory.

Gertrude the Great
ESS VI
A meditation on praise and thanksgiving

To have and to hold

Here I come to you, the one I have loved,
the one in whom I have believed,
the one I have chosen to cherish.

You are the joy of my spirit,
you are the praise of my heart and my mouth,
my Jesus!
I will follow you wherever you go.
Since you have claimed my heart for yourself,
and taken her for your own possession,
never, in all eternity, can you be taken away from me.

Here I come to you, the one I have loved,
the one in whom I have believed,
the one I have chosen to cherish.

My beloved, my Jesus,
I draw you close to my heart
in love's embrace which knows no separation.
Here and now I have you,
held by all the love of my heart!
And even if you bless me a thousand times,
I will never let you go.

Gertrude the Great
ESS IV
A meditation on religious profession
cf Gen 32:26; Rom 8:38-39

Open to love

Come, Jesus, dearest love of my heart,
I know no spiritual fruit can grow
until it is drenched with the dew of your Spirit
and warmed with the power of your love.

Show me your tenderness, then,
take me in the arms of your love,
and warm me through and through with your Spirit!
Here is my body and soul:
I give it all to you that you may have me.

My dearest Love,
pour your blessing into me.
Open yourself to me
and draw me into the fullness of your sweetness.
For I long for you with all my heart and soul;
I pray that you alone should have me.
Then I shall be yours and you shall be mine.
Let me grow in your life-giving love
with the ever new warmth of your Spirit,
and, by your grace, I shall blossom
like lilies of the valley beside streams of water.

Gertrude the Great
ESS II
A prayer for the anniversary of a nun taking the habit

The indwelling of love

O fragrant oil of God's own excellence,
swelling the streams of love on every side,
surging and flourishing throughout eternity,
yet, in the limits of earthly time, poured out
    everywhere!
O the overwhelming power of the Most High
when such a frail vessel, depressed in the shame of
    sin,
comes upon such a precious liquid dwelling within!
O clearest, truest witness
that God abounds in faithful love!

Though I strayed so long in sin's lonely haunts,
you have not withdrawn from me,
but stayed within me
so that the sweetness of our happy union
might be shown to me in the measure of my
understanding!

Gertrude the Great
LDP II.6
A meditation on receiving Christ at Christmas

Love me deeply

The soul:

> Come, Lord,
> love me deeply,
> love me often and love me long!
> For the more often you love me,
> the purer I become;
> the more deeply you love me,
> the more beautiful I become;
> the longer you love me,
> the holier I become here on earth.

God:

> I love you often,
> because it is my nature,
> for I am Love myself.
> I love you deeply,
> because it is my desire,
> for I long for everyone to love me deeply.
> I love you long,
> because I am eternal,
> for I have no end.

Mechthild of Magdeburg
VLG I.23-24

The school of love

My Love, my God,
the only way to make progress here
is to follow you totally
and love you alone unceasingly.
Let me not be left behind in the school of your love...
but in you and through you and with you,
let me progress day by day from strength to strength
and so bear fruit for you, my Love,
in the new vineyard of your love.

Gertrude the Great
ESS V
A prayer for the Office of Sext
from a meditation on Arousing the love of God

I hold you by love

I hold you by love, most loving Jesus,
and I will not let you go,
for your blessing will never be enough for me
unless I hold you
and keep you as my best part, all my hope and
    longing.
O Love, life-giving Life,
you are the living word of God: bring me to life.
Whatever of God's love is broken or extinguished,
repair in me by your grace.

My Love, my God, you created me:
recreate me by your love.
O Love, you redeemed me:
whatever of your love has been neglected in me,
supply from yourself and redeem in me.
My Love, my God, you gained me for yourself by the
    blood of your Christ:
make me holy in your truth.

My Love, my God, you have adopted me as a
    daughter:
feed, O feed me next to your heart.
O Love, you chose me for yourself and for no other:
make me cling to you with all my being.
My Love, my God, you have loved me freely:
make me love you with all my heart, all my soul and
    all my strength.

O Love, most powerful God: strengthen me by your
    love.
O Love, most wise: let me love you wisely.
O Love, most sweet: let me taste you sweetly.
O Love, most dear: let me live for you alone.
O Love, most faithful: comfort and support me in
    every trouble.
O Love, most companionable: be the doer of all my
    deeds.
O Love, most victorious: let me persevere with you to
    the end.

Gertrude the Great
ESS V
A meditation on Arousing the love of God
cf Gen 32:26

Parting

Lord, I come before you as a naked soul,
And you are, by nature, God in glorious array.
But our communion with each other
Is eternal life without death's decay.
This brings a blessed sense of peace, quiet and still,
To each will.
You give yourself to me and I give myself for ever.
What has happened to me now I know well,
In this I find my comfort.

But as for this happiness, time passing may discover,
Where two lovers come secretly together,
Though inseparable, each must often leave the other.

Dear friend of God, I have described for you love's
    art:
God must teach it to your heart.

Mechthild of Magdeburg
VLG I.44

Absence

Dear Lord, how still is your silence –
But I will always thank you for your long absence.
Your glorious praise will always shine,
Now that your will is done, not mine.
So I will put my trust in the word
I have heard in your Gospel, Christ,
When you say, 'Whoever loves me I will love;
My Father and I will come to them
And we will make our home with them.'
Give me, then, your loving kindness, Lord!
You cannot deny me.

Our Lord replied:
'When the moment I judge proper comes
For me to give you the gifts of heaven,
Then I will be quick to act.
At the ready my eternal power I hold,
And in time my purpose will unfold,
And I will raise you up from blood-stained earth,
Nothing can rank for me of greater worth.

Mechthild of Magdeburg
VLG VII.46
cf Jn 14:23

Resting in love

My Love, my God,
you are my dearest possession,
without you I have no hope nor desire
in heaven or in earth.
You are my true inheritance
and all the longing of my life and thought.

My Love,
let the goal of my life
be your pleasure consummated in me!
Show me that covenant of marriage
in which my heart joins with yours.
Show me, as evening draws on,
for you are the light of the evening sky,
the light I see in the face of my dear God.
My Evening Star, dearest and brightest of all,
graciously appear to me at my death,
that I may have the Evening Star of my desire,
and gently fall asleep in all your fullest sweetness,
and find rest in my heart.

Come, fount of eternal light,
take me to yourself from whom I came.
There may I know as I am known,
and love as I am loved,
that I may see you as you are, my God,
and, seeing you, enjoy you and possess you
for evermore.

Gertrude the Great
ESS V
A prayer for the Office of Vespers
from a meditation on Arousing the love of God
cf 1 Cor 13:12

In need

For help to repent

Dear Lord, I pray
That you will come to me in my need
As my dearest Friend of all;
Make me truly sorry for all my sin
And all my guilt will be erased within,
That, when this earthly life is past,
I may live untroubled at the last.

Mechthild of Magdeburg
VLG VII.35
Prayers on the seven penitential psalms:
Ps 32(31)

Prayer for forgiveness

Jesus Christ,
guide us with your boundless compassion
and compel us with your perfect love
to live according to your will
in the truth.
By your holy passion
forgive all the evil we have done
in thought, in word, in deed,
and in all the good we have neglected to do in our
    life.
Give us the power to overcome all human evil,
as the love of your dear heart grows within us.
By the power of your five holy wounds, I pray,
give us the pure truth,
imprint it upon us and absorb us in it,
that the truth may live in us
and we in the truth.

Margaret Ebner
Off. 50b

91

Just as I am

Help me,
Lord my God.

By God's grace
I am what I am.

Elisabeth of Schönau
Visiones I.10
cf 1 Cor 15:10

Love conquers all

The Soul:

Lord, my guilt, through which I have lost you,
Stands before my eyes like a great mountain.
It has brought deep darkness between me and you
And created an eternal distance from you and me.
Come then, my Love, loved above all others,
Draw me back to you...

Lord, my life here stands before my eyes
Like an arid field
Where little good has grown.
Come then, sweet Jesus Christ,
Send me now the sweet rain of your humanity,
The hot sun of your life-giving Godhead,
And the soft dew of the Holy Spirit,
That I may confess the sorrow of my heart.

Lord, your eternal kingdom stands open to my eyes
Like the noblest wedding, the greatest marriage,
And the longest companionship.
Come then, my Love,
And take your longing bride
To be yours for ever!

God:

Your mountain shall melt in love,
Your enemies shall have no part in your reward,
Your field has felt the hot sun scorching it,
Yet your fruit has stayed unspoilt.
In my kingdom there will be a new bride.
There I will give you the sweet kiss of my mouth
That all my Godhead may soar through your soul
And my loving gaze play unceasingly upon your
heart.
What is left of your sorrow then?
For though you prayed for a thousand years,
I would not cause you any sighs or fears.

Mechthild of Magdeburg
VLG IV.5

In great need

O great Father,
We are in great need:
So we call on you to hear us now.
Hear us for the sake of your Son,
The Word through whom you have made us abound
In all the things we lack.
Now, Father, let it be your will,
As it is your nature,
To look on us in mercy and bring us your help,
That we may not fail
Nor let your Name be hidden
In our darkness.
By the power of your Name
Have mercy and come to our help!

Hildegard of Bingen
SACR 1

In despair

Lord Jesus Christ, look on this poor soul of mine,
I flee to you, I long for you to help,
For my enemies hunt me down.
Lord God, I pour out all my pain to you:
They would blot me out of your sight.
Lord, Son of God almighty, blot them out for me!
Do not hand me over to their power,
But keep me pure in you,
For you have redeemed me by your passion.
Be now my help and comfort, Lord,
And do not let me perish,
For it was your will to die for me.
Lord Jesus Christ, I seek your help.
Wake my soul up from her lazy sleep
And let your light release me from the darkness of my
    flesh.
Be my companion and my guide
That I may journey on my way to you,
As far as may be, without falling into sin,
For you see all that I do wrong.

Mary, Queen of heaven, Mother of God's own seed,
Come to my help with all your speed,
For in the sorrow of my sin I am in need
Of finding grace
Before your dear Son's face.
Mother of all holiness,
I pour out to you all my heartfelt sadness.

Mechthild of Magdeburg
VLG VII.26

For sinners

Sweet Father,
with all the blessings of your love,
I praise you for all your faithful care
for my poor body and soul.
With all these blessings,
I thank you, great God,
for all the kind gifts you have ever given my body and
    soul.
With the whole community of all your creatures
I long to praise you, Father, from my heart
in everything and for everything
which has flowed perfect from your sweet heart.
But with all these blessings, Lord,
my dearest prayer of all
is for sinners who languish in their sins today:
give them a true change of heart,
help them to repent in full,
and give you the glory.

Mechthild of Magdeburg
VLG V.35

For healing

I pray to you, Lord,
for the healing of your holiness,
the protection of your truth,
and the full indwelling of your Holy Spirit
for all those I name before you,
who, through your love, have helped me in my need
to bear my present sorrows in body and soul.
God of all riches,
through the poverty of your Son Jesus,
change the pain of my spiritual poverty

and the gall of my bitterness
into honey on the palate of my soul.
Living God,
teach us the eternal excellence of our Christian faith,
and keep us from all wrong ways with your godly
     wisdom.
And make our spirit stand firm, Lord,
that it may find rest in your Holy Trinity.

Mechthild of Magdeburg
VLG V.35

Thanksgiving in sickness

Lord, I thank you:
>   in your love you have taken all earthly riches away
>   from me,
>   that you may clothe and feed me
>   through the kindness of strangers.
>   Now everything that might clothe my heart
>   with the pride of possession
>   is estranged from me.

Lord, I thank you:
>   you have taken the strength of my eyesight away
>   from me,
>   that you may serve me now through the eyes of
>   strangers.

Lord, I thank you:
>   you have taken the strength of my hands away from
>   me,
>   that you may serve me now through the hands of
>   strangers.

Lord, I thank you:
  you have taken the strength of my heart away from
      me,
  that you may serve me now through the hearts of
      strangers.

Lord, I pray for them all:
  reward them on earth
  with your heavenly love,
  that they may be strong for you
  in prayer and service,
  and come to a holy death.

Mechthild of Magdeburg
VLG VII.64

The powerful and the powerless

Dear Lord,
I pray for all who persecute my fellow Christians:
let them know you more nearly and love you more
    truly.

God of all power,
I pray for false leaders in government:
stir them up with truth and understanding.
I pray for the vulnerable in the community:
may they find forbearance and compassion.

Eternal Comforter,
I pray for all troubled souls:
come to them now and comfort them;
take away from them all fear for their life;
God of compassion, guard them and keep them,
and bring them to eternal life.

Lord,
I pray for all those who have the spiritual strength of
   your love,
whom I name before you now:
cleanse them, encourage them to stand firm,
and help them live your way of truth in everything
for your praise.

God of all kindness,
make us truly thankful at all times
for all your gifts
that help those who bear heavy burdens
to bear them with your love.

Mechthild of Magdeburg
VLG V.35

Mother Church

The bride of Christ

O burning light of heaven's starry height,
O bright bride of this royal wedding night,
O dazzling jewel,
You are arrayed in noble apparel,
For you have no sin nor stain!
You are a close companion of the angel band,
A citizen with all saints in the promised land.
Flee away from the ancient tempter's lair,
And come into the palace of your King so fair!

Hildegard of Bingen
SACR 68
cf Ps 45(44):9-15
Eph 5:27

Mother Church

Now may the womb of Mother Church quicken with
    joy,
For in heavenly harmony
Her children have been gathered to her breast!
Therefore, foulest snake of Satan,
You are confounded.
For those you thought you held in your maw
Now shine, cleansed by the blood of God's own Son.
And so the praise is yours,
King most high!
Alleluia!

Hildegard of Bingen
SACR 57

God's jewel

O Church of immeasurable might,
God-girt with armour for faith's fight,
Bejewelled with gems of jacinth bright,
You are the fragrance bringing
Wounded nations healing,
City of all science and learning!
You are christened and consecrated
With soaring songs of praise:
You are a precious stone of burning light!

Hildegard of Bingen
SACR 67
For the dedication of a church
Cf Apoc 21:16-22:2

The Church in need

O eternal God,
Let your love for us burn within you;
So may we be the same members of your Son's body
That you first made us to be in your love
When you begot your Son at the dawn of time
Before creation was yet made.
Look on this need which has befallen us,
Take it from us for the sake of your Son,
And lead us to the joy of your salvation.

Hildegard of Bingen
SACR 2

The feast of love

Preparing

Come now, dear Lord, I pray,
As a faithful confessor to a dear friend,
And bring me the true light, your Holy Spirit's gift,
That I may see and know myself through and through,
And mourn all my sins from deep within my heart.
With such a hope of holiness
May my spirit find a cure
From all my sins' past lure
That I may at length be found most pure.
Then give me, Lord, your own body,
That I may, my dearest Lord,receive you
With a love as great
As human heart can contemplate.
Then you may for evermore remain
Food for the journey of my poor soul's pain.
So may I, dear Lord, your life-companion remain
With you in everlasting life and love to reign.

Mechthild of Magdeburg
VLG VII.35
Prayers on the seven penitential psalms: Ps 38(37)

Longing

Come, my Love, my God,
you are my one true love,
you are my saving health, all my hope and all my joy,
my highest and my greatest good!
I wait and watch for you this morning,
my God, my dearest Love,
for you are always pleasure and sweetness.
For you my heart thirsts and you alone can satisfy my
spirit;

the more I taste you, the more I hunger,
the more I drink, the more I thirst.

My Love, my God,
to see you is my brightest day,
the day which is better spent in the Lord's house
than a thousand other days,
the day for which my soul is longing,
the soul which you have redeemed to be yours.
Come and satisfy me with the sweetness of your
    honeyed lips,
for I want and need the rich taste of your pleasure.

My Love, to see you is to rise in thought to God,
to cling to you is to be wedded one with God.
My soul's clearest light, my morning's brightest light,
let your light dawn upon me and within me now,
that in your light I may see light,
and through you my night be turned to day.
Come, my dearest Morning Light,
against your love let me write off all that is not you.
Visit me now at the first light of day,
and let me be changed, suddenly, wholly into you.

Gertrude the Great
ESS V
A morning prayer from a meditation on
Arousing the love of God
cf Ps 84(83); 36(35):8-9

At love's breast

Come, my Love,
prepare the feast of your tender-hearted breast,
and invite me to the table of your sweets:
set before me the sweetest dish of your eternal
    forgiveness
which alone can strengthen my spirit.

Let us feast together,
my dearest and my greatest good!
In every good thing you flow and overflow
    immeasurably,
and share yourself wonderfully
in communion with your creation.
Refresh me generously,
for you are my food!

Come and let the fire of your love
totally consume me, spirit and soul together,
for it is this almighty power of yours,
so generously given,
that has had such effect on this speck of dust!
My Love, my sweetest noonday heat,
your leisure delights me above all else
with peace in all its fullness.

Come, my Beloved, loved and beloved above all
    creation,
show me how I may find you;
tell me where you feed and where you lie resting at
    noon.
See how my spirit warms and burns
for the sweetness of sharing your leisure!

Gertrude the Great
ESS V
A midday prayer from a meditation
on Arousing the love of God
cf Song of Songs 1:7

The bread of angels

Arise, my soul, arise,
it is good to rejoice and join the angels' praises,
it is our health and strength to share in God's own
    feast!

For this is the bread of angels,
the living bread come down from heaven,
the bread which strengthens the human heart,
that we may live in the flesh –
not in the way of the flesh but in the way of the Spirit.

O manna, unknown to mortal eyes,
overflowing goodness that suckles earth's living
    creatures,
fullest sweetness of the angels,
delightful food of all the blessed!
O welcome refreshment,
bringing with you such a happy company!
You know no harm and bear all pain,
you forgive sinners and refresh the dying,
you repel the powers of the enemy,
you guide those returning from earth to heaven,
you kill death and offer life for ever.

Blessed are the eyes that see you,
O purest light, O sweetest beauty!
Blessed are the hearts that love you,
O love that quenches all thirst, O sweetness that keeps
    us safe!
Blessed are those who hunger and thirst for you,
but more blessed are they in every way
who, once satisfied by you,
neither hunger nor thirst for all eternity.

Elisabeth of Schönau
GB XV
cf Jn 6:50-51

The drink Christ drank

I am sick and I long for a health-giving drink,
The drink that Jesus Christ drank
When he came, human and divine, into that crib
And found the drink we had all ready for him.
From that drink he drank so much
That he was drunk, so heady with the fire of love
That he bore all the suffering of his heart with every
    grace:
He always gave graces which are good and never
    unhealthy!

For this health-giving drink I long,
Yet it is a painful drink of bitter herbs
Because of all God's loving.
So bitter is the pain,
Let us add another herb – the will to suffer gladly.
The second herb is patience in pain,
And that is bitter too.
So let us add another herb – devotion of the heart,
Which sweetens patience and all our work.
The third ingredient is long-suffering in pain and hope
For our eternal life and saving health.
That is very bitter too.
So let us add another herb – unwearied joy.

Come then, dear Lord, give me this drink, I pray,
That, in unwearied joy, no pain may me dismay.
Then I would heaven itself awhile delay,
So sweet is my desire for this.
Now let it be your will and pleasure, Lord, to make
This gift to me and all who seek it for love's sake.

Mechthild of Magdeburg
VLG VII.33
cf. Mk 10:35-40

Jesus my all

Jesus, my beloved creator,
Jesus, my beloved redeemer,
Jesus, my beloved sustainer!

You are my hope,
    my food,
    my trust,
    my comfort,
and all my desire!

Lord my God,
now make my soul grow
and open wide my heart!

Dorothea of Montau
Sept. III.11

Stay with me

Jesus Christ, my beloved Lord,
immerse yourself in my soul!
Jesus Christ, best of all,
whoever has you in the heart
is known to have fine guests!
All-powerful, only-begotten Son of God,
how great is your grace and your love!

O all-powerful, eternal Son of God,
stay with me;
do not let me be exiled alone in sadness,
but stay with me day and night!
O all-powerful, eternal, sweet Lord Jesus Christ,
stay with me,
and make your great feast in my soul!

110

Lord Jesus Christ,
feed me and revive me with your warmth,
for my soul burns with thirst and hunger for you.
Beloved Lord Jesus Christ,
bless me with the dew of heaven,
bless me with the richness of the earth,
bless me with the blessing of the Holy Spirit!

Dorothea of Montau
Sept. III.27
cf Lk 24:13-35

The food of eternity

Blessed are you, Lord Jesus Christ,
God of the living God,
Son praised for your love!
Now I know for certain that you are really present
    here,
truly human and divine...

Lord Jesus Christ,
by your holy death and painful passion,
by your holy body suffering on the cross,
look upon all my need and my last end
with the eyes of your divine compassion,
with the faithfulness of your humanity,
and with the favour of your Holy Spirit.
Then give me, Lord, your own body,
that I may receive you with such Christian faith and
    heartfelt love
that your holy body may always be
the last food of my body and the eternal bread of my
    poor soul.

Mechthild of Magdeburg
VLG VI.37

The peace of Christ

May your sacred body and your precious blood,
my Lord Jesus Christ,
keep my body and soul in eternal life.
May your peace be with me.
In you, Jesus, our true Peace,
let me have for all eternity peace upon peace,
that through you I may reach that peace
which passes all understanding,
where I may see you in the joy of eternity.

Gertrude the Great
ESS I
A prayer at communion when commemorating our baptism
cf Phil 4:7

A new beginning

O Jesus, my soul's sweetest host,
my heart's dearest treasure!
May your sweet union of my body with your body
be for me today the forgiveness of all my sins,
the repairing of all my omissions,
and the recovery of my lost life.
Be my eternal salvation, the restoring of my body and
    soul,
the kindling of love, the renewal of grace,
and the eternal enfolding of my life within you.

Be my freedom of the spirit,
the health of my life and the honesty of my behaviour.
Be my shield of patience, my badge of humility,
my staff of confidence, my comfort in sadness,
my help to persevere.

Be my armour of faith, my kernel of hope,
my perfection of love, my fulfilling of your
    commandments,
the renewing of my spirit, my consecration in the
    truth,
and the consummation of my whole religion.

Be my source of all grace,
the end of my failings, the growth of all goodness,
and the continual witness of your love in me.
So, in this bodily journey,
let my thoughts be always turned to you, my best part,
and, at my life's end, let me reach that sweetest prize.
There, in the new constellation of your glorified
    humanity,
I shall see the brightest light of your awesome
    Godhead.
There, stripped of the troubles of this life,
I shall feast, full of joy for all eternity,
and rejoice in the riches of your love,
as a bride rejoices in the pleasures of her king!

Gertrude the Great
ESS I
A prayer at communion when commemorating our baptism

Our Mother's food

'O that you were like a brother to me,
that sucked my mother's breasts!
Then, if I found you outside,
I would kiss you and no one would despise me.'

I call you my brother,
because you took our flesh yourself,
yet you suck the tender heart of truth,

the food with which the Godhead nourishes humanity:
she is my Mother, for she created me,
and she gives me life through nature's growth.
The food of the Church is also full of your grace:
you offer her your full richness to suckle
in the sacrament of your body and blood,
for you are the living bread
and the fount of living water!

Hildegard of Bingen
Scivias II.6
cf Song of Songs 8:1

The cradle of the heart

Let us come with joy and heartfelt love,
Open our soul to receive our Love,
And, as into a sweetly restful cradle,
Lay within our soul our dearest Love,
Whose glory in lullaby of praise we sing
For that first plight so willingly endured,
When Christ lay there in the crib.
Let us kneel before our Love
In body and in soul, and say:
Lord, I thank you for yourself!
Now, dearest Love, grant my prayer,
Give me the treasure of your heart,
Let my life be free from sin in every part...
My lap is here, my Lord, for you to rest,
Your pillow my heart's sorrow ready for her Guest,
My bed's coverlet is my all-enfolding longing
To see pardoned sinners quicken my rejoicing.
Now, Lord, as we lie so close together,
Let us pledge our love, each to the other.

Mechthild of Magdeburg
VLG VII.21

Lovers in eternity

The Virgin Mary

O noble, bounteous and glorious
Maiden untouched, we greet you!
You are the pupil in the eye of chastity,
The womb of holiness, matter of sanctity,
For you were pleasing to God!

In you this heavenly drink was poured,
The Word clothed in your flesh all flesh restored;
You are the lily of dazzling whiteness
Whom God regarded above all creation!

O most beautiful, most sweet,
How powerfully God found delight and joy in you,
Embracing you with warmth,
And coming within you
So that God's Son might be suckled with your milk.

Your womb indeed cherished joy and gladness,
When heaven's harmony rang out for you in
     happiness.
For you, a virgin, bore the Son of God
Where your chastity shone clear in God's holiness.

Your body cherished joy deep within,
As grass when dew falls,
Drenching it with green freshness:
So it was done in you,
Mother of all joy!

Now let the whole Church rise like dawn with joy,
Ring our her praise and all her harmony employ
To honour Mary, sweetest Virgin,
Worthy of our every hymn,
Birth-giver of God! Amen.

Hildegard of Bingen
SACR 12

Mother of creation

O greenest Stem, we greet you,
For in the gusty breeze of the quest of the saints
You gave birth!

When the time came
For you to flower on your branches –
O how we welcome you for that coming! –
The warmth of the Sun exuded within you
A perfume like the oil of balsam.

For in you flowered a flower of beauty
Which gave all spices their perfume
When they were parched dry.
And they have all appeared
In the green of their full freshness.

So the skies bedewed the pastures,
And all the earth was made glad,
Because her womb brought forth wheat
And the birds of the sky made their nests in her.

And now a feast has been prepared for humankind,
And great rejoicing of banqueters.
Therefore, O sweet Virgin,
In you there is no joy lacking!

All this Eve despised...
But now all praise to God most high!

Hildegard of Bingen
SACR 71
cf Is 45:8

Nursing Mother

Save us, Mary, Queen of mercy,
oil of tender-heartedness:
through you has come the medicine of life,
Queen of mercy, Virgin Mother of the divine seed;
through you has come the race of heavenly light,
the seed of Israel's fragrance.

Through your Son you have become the true mother
    of all,
for God did not disdain to become our brother:
come, then, for the love of Christ,
take me in my unworthiness into the care of your
    motherhood;
support, sustain and equip my faith,
and so become the nursing mother of my renewal and
    my faith
that you may be for evermore my own dearly loved
    mother,
always faithfully caring for me in this life,
until, at the hour of death,
you take me into the fullness of your motherhood.

Gertrude the Great
ESS I
A meditation on baptism

The milk of grace

Lady, as you suckled once,
so suckle still
martyrs with strong faith in their hearts,
penitents with holy warnings in their ears,
virgins with your purity,
widows with steadfastness,

oppressors with compassion,
sinners with prayers of repentance.

Lady, you can suckle us still,
for your breasts are still so full –
you cannot restrain them.
Will you then not suckle me,
though your milk may bring you much pain?
For I have seen your breasts so full
that seven streams pour forth all at once from one
   breast
upon my body and soul.
In that vision you gave me a work to do
which no friend of God can bear without sorrow in
   the heart.
As you will suckle still until the last day,
so you must be emptied
if God's children and your children are to be weaned
and grow to full, eternal life.
Thereafter, in unbounded pleasure let us know and
   see the milk
from that same breast which Jesus often kissed.

Mechthild of Magdeburg
VLG I.22

Prophets of fire

O fruitful roots!
In you God planted the work of miracles
And not the work of sin;
You have grown through a stormy, shadowy
   pilgrimage,
Shot through with light.
And you, John the Baptist,
Are the fiery voice that feeds on God's word,

Heralding the cornerstone
That polishes all other stones and overturns hell's
    abyss,
Rejoice in Christ your Head!
Rejoice!
For many are they who never saw Christ on earth,
Yet called upon the Lord with the fire of faith.
Rejoice in Christ your Head!

Hildegard of Bingen
SACR 23

John the Baptist

Holy John, forerunner and herald of the King of
    peace,
Baptist of the spotless Lamb,
bring me the help of the Holy Spirit,
with which you were so wonderfully filled
through all your life from your mother's womb.

You are the greatest hermit,
a mirror of the life that is given to God alone,
pray to the Lord for me.
May God's generous forgiveness blot out all the dirt of
    sin in me
and keep me safe from the pollution of every
    impurity.
Let the welcome fire of God's love with all its message
be poured into the depth of my heart and kindled in
    my bones;
let my thoughts and works be guided
in the right path of the Lord's commandments
by your prayers,
for you were chosen to prepare the way of Christ.

I come to you, I cry to you in prayer,
precious martyr, rose red in grace, pearl of heaven,
blessed John, hear me and pray for me.
May my name be written in the book of life,
may the Lord count me among the children of God's
    choice
in the building of the heavenly Jerusalem,
and may my mouth be filled with the perfect praise of
    God.

Elisabeth of Schönau
GB IV
Cf Lk 1:41-44, 3:1-17

Apostles of light

O shining company of apostles,
Towering in true knowledge!
You unlocked the door of the devil's domain
By washing its captives clean
In the fountain of living water.
You are the brightest light in pitch darkness,
The bravest race, pillars of the world,
Upholding the Bride of the Lamb
With all her jewels of grace.
To the joy of the Lamb
She who is both Mother and Virgin
Has raised her banner of victory high,
For the spotless Lamb is the Bridegroom of the
    spotless Bride.

Hildegard of Bingen
SACR 25
cf Apoc 3:7-13, 21:9-14

John the Evangelist

O mirror of the Holy Dove in purest form!
You have gazed into the mystic depth
In the fountain of clearest water,
How wonderful is your flowering
Which never dried up and withered,
For the heavenly Gardener planted you.
O sweet repose of the Sun's embraces,
You are the special son of the Lamb
Within a chosen people's bond of friendship,
The new strain of God's planting.

Hildegard of Bingen
SACR 26
Cf Jn 13:23; 15:1-8

Virgins of the sun

O noblest life,
Lush in your fresh green growth!
You take root in the warmth of the Sun,
You shine in dazzling brightness
In the circle of light
Which no earthly excellence can comprehend:
You are enfolded in the embrace of God's mysteries!
You glow red as the dawn
And burn as the flame of the Sun!

Hildegard of Bingen
SACR 39

Martyrs of the Lamb

O victorious conquerors!
By the shedding of your blood
You have kept the building up of the Church
Safe and sound.
You have entered the covenant of the blood of the
    Lamb,
Feasting on the food of the one who was slain.
How great is your reward,
For you regarded your bodily life so lightly!
You followed the Lamb of God,
And adorned the sacrifice of Christ,
Who by such a death has brought you
Into your restored inheritance!

Hildegard of Bingen
SACR 31

The communion of saints

I praise you and adore you,
I worship your greatness and your glory,
and I bless you, good Jesus!
Beyond all telling was your joy
when God the Father granted your desire
that all your friends should have an inheritance
for all eternity.
And so, that kindest prayer of yours was fulfilled:
'Father, I want my servants to be there too, where I
    am.'
For you wanted every joy and every good thing
which you are yourself
to be theirs for ever.

By that joy beyond all telling, I pray:
Loving mediator between humanity and God,
let me share that blessed fellowship of all your chosen
    people,
that I may have you together with them,
for you are the one and only joy
and all that is good, here and in all eternity.

Mechtild of Hackeborn
LSG I.19
cf Jn 12:26, 17:24

The praises of heaven

Lord almighty, God-with-us,
Before all time our Parent, God, begot you,
And in time the Virgin Mother bore you.
Your own twofold nature wonderfully endues you
As the Christ, the one and only true:
Though diverse in nature, you do not divide your
    unity,
And though one person, you do not deny diversity.
For your glory shining hosts of angels sing for joy,
And the distant stars sweet harmony employ;
For your praise each known thing brings its
    knowledge,
All created matter pays her homage!
Following the Father's will and in the Spirit's unity,
You became a human being, sharing vulnerable
    humanity,
Yet you save us by the power of God's invulnerability.
This you did that none who trust in you might fall,
But that all believers should for ever live the life
    eternal.

Therefore, you did not disdain to taste our death's
  dark night,
And destroyed our death by your own resurrection's
  might!

Hroswith (Roswitha) of Gandersheim
Sapientia IX

Sources

Latin sources:

Hroswith	P	Poésies Latines de Roswith, *Paris 1854*
		Sapientia' from Hroswithae Opera, *ed. H. Homeyer, München 1970.*
Hildegard of Bingen	GB	Gebetbuch, *Faks-Ausgabe des Codex Latinus Monacensis 935 der Bayerischen Staatsbibliothek*
	LDO	Liber Divinorum Operum.
		'Scivias' J.P. Migne, Patrologia Latina *197, 1855*
	SACR	Symphonia Armoniae Celestium Revelationum *ed. Pudentiana-Barth, Salzburg 1969*
Elisabeth of Schönau	GB	Das Gebetbuch der hl. Elisabeth von Schönau, *ed. F. Roth, Augsburg 1886*
		Die Visionen der heiligen Elisabeth und die Schrifter der Äbte Ekbert und Emecho von Schönau, *ed. Roth, Brünn 1884*
Mechtild of Hackeborn	LSG	Liber Specialis Gratiae
		Revelationes Gertrudianae ac Mechtildianae, *ed. Solesmes, Paris 1875-77*
Gertrude the Great	ESS	Exercitia Spiritualia Septem
	LDP	Legatus Divinae Pietatis, *ed. Solesmes, Paris 1875-77*
Dorothea of Montau	Sept.	Septililium beatae Dorotheae Montoviensis, *ed. Joannes Marienwerder, Brussels 1885*

127

German sources:

Mechthild
of Magdeburg   VLG   Ein Vliessendes Licht der Gotheit. Offenbarungen
                       der Schwester Mechthild von Magdeburg, *ed. P*
                       Gall Morel, Regensburg 1869; reprint: Darmstadt
                       1976

Elisabeth
Staeglin   VHS   Vita Henrici Susonis
                       Heinrich Seuse-Deutsche Schriften, ed. K
                       Bihlmeyer, Stuttgart 1907; reprint: Frankfurt 1971

Margaret
Ebner   Off.   Offenbarungen, *ed. P. Strauch, Freiburg i.Br.*
                       1882.

FOR FURTHER READING

Bowie F., Beguine Spirituality, *SPCK, London 1989*
Bowie F./Davies O., Hildegard of Bingen: An Anthology, *SPCK, London*
    1990
Bynum, C.W., Jesus as Mother, *University of California 1982*
Flanagan S., Hildegard of Bingen: A Visionary Life, *Routledge, London*
    1989
Labarge, M.W., A Small Sound of the Trumpet: Women in Mediaeval Life,
    Hamish Hamilton 1986, 1990
Newman B., 'Sister of Wisdom', St Hildegard's Theology of the Feminine,
    Scolar Press, Aldershot 1987
Shank L.T./Nichols J.A. (eds.), Mediaeval Religious Women:
    Peaceweavers, *Cistercian Publications, Michigan 1987*

Index